THE WISDOM
OF BALSEKAR

Ramesh S. Balsekar is known and loved by seekers from around the world as an eloquent Master of Advaita, or non-duality. After retiring as President of the Bank of India, Ramesh translated many of the daily talks given in the Marathi language by his Guru, Nisargadatta Maharaj. Ramesh's teaching began in 1982 after Maharaj had twice directed him to talk, and since then he has written over twenty books on Advaita.

Alan Jacobs, a retired businessman and art dealer, has made a life-long study of mysticism. He has also made an extensive study of the teachings of G. I. Gurdjieff, J. Krishnamurti and Douglas Harding, and is Chairman of the Ramana Maharshi Foundation in the UK. He is a poet himself and is published regularly. He lives in London.

THE WISDOM
OF BALSEKAR

**The Essence of Enlightenment from the
World's Leading Teacher of Advaita**

**EDITED BY ALAN JACOBS
FOREWORD BY WAYNE LIQUORMAN**

WATKINS PUBLISHING

LONDON

This edition published in the UK in 2004 by
Watkins Publishing, Sixth Floor, Castle House,
75–76 Wells Street, London, W1T 3QH

© Ramesh S. Balsekar and Alan Jacobs 2004

Ramesh S. Balsekar and Alan Jacobs have asserted their rights under
the Copyright, Designs and Patents Act, 1988, to be identified as
authors of this work.

Designed and typeset by Jerry Goldie
Printed and bound in Great Britain
British Library Cataloguing in Publication data available
Library of Congress Cataloguing in Publication data available

ISBN 1 84293 079 6

www.watkinspublishing.com

To all those men and women who are called
to earnestly seek the Truth

CONTENTS

ACKNOWLEDGEMENTS

To Ramesh Balsekar for his cooperation in the original writing of this book and for correcting and approving the final manuscript.

To Wayne Liquorman for giving permission to use extracts from the Ramesh books published by Advaita Press, writing the foreword and checking the textual entries.

To Mrs Chhaya Arya for giving permission to use extracts from *Experience of Immortality* published by Chetana Publishers.

To Yogesh for giving permission to use extracts from all Ramesh's books published by Zen Publishers.

To Catharine Pye for painstakingly typing the manuscript.

To Annie Wilson for her editorial assistance.

To Michael Mann for suggesting a Ramesh Balsekar anthology.

FOREWORD

Love ... The love of Total Acceptance. This is the heart of the Teaching and nowhere does it shine more brightly or more clearly than in the words of Ramesh S. Balsekar.

You hold in your hands a distillation of nearly two decades of Ramesh's efforts to dispel the darkness and illuminate the mystery. For those of us privileged to have been intimate with this great Sage and his words, Ramesh's Teaching has come alive as a living entity. It is a Teaching devoid of compromise ... at once complex and utterly simple. It is a Teaching that challenges our most fundamental notions about who we are and the nature of the universe we appear to inhabit. We are affected, moved, transformed.

Throughout these pages are to be found countless pointers to a profound Truth, a singular Truth ... a Truth that is vast and Unknowable and yet as familiar and intimate as our breath.

I consider myself privileged and blessed to have had the opportunity to edit several of Ramesh's books. The fruits of some of that labor are extracted here. Through the years of working intimately with his words I came to appreciate the incredible depth of his genius and awesome breadth of his compassion.

There is no greater challenge than to attempt to codify the Infinite, to describe the Indescribable. In fact, it is a task doomed to failure. Yet there is something heroic and inspirational in Ramesh's unflinching attempt to do the impossible. The ultimate result of this undertaking is a body of work that can properly be called wisdom ... the Wisdom of Ramesh S. Balsekar.

Wayne Liquorman
Hermosa Beach, California, 2002

INTRODUCTION

Sri Ramesh Sadashiv Balsekar, born in Mumbai on 25 May 1917, is undoubtedly the world's leading living teacher of Advaita, and the Indian philosophy of non-dualism, 'not two but one'.

This magnificent teaching stems from the later Upanishads and was codified by the great 11th-century sage, Acharya Shankara, in his commentary on the Brahmana Sutras. In the 20th century a renaissance of Advaita occurred through the exemplary life, teaching, and powerful silent Presence of Sri Bhagavan Ramana Maharshi (1896–1950), Sage of Aronachala, Tiruvannamalai, in Southern India.

Ramesh has said on many occasions that his primary inspiration for exploring the spiritual life came from Ramana Maharshi. He regards himself as a devotee of Ramana to continue the work and I have personally heard him say in Mumbai that he endeavours to give the advanced exposition of the teaching of Ramana Maharshi. Every morning, seven days a week, before his talks, he pays obeisance to a portrait of Ramana Maharshi. Another portrait hangs behind him from the chair where he talks to questioners from all over the world, as he has done for over twenty years.

His following is worldwide. Thousands have enjoyed meeting this wise Sage and spiritual Master who courteously answers their questions with great heartfelt compassion and then fires finely honed arrows of truth straight into their hearts with unerring accuracy.

Ramana Maharshi taught largely through silence. He did however answer many questions, which have been faithfully recorded in *Talks* (three volumes) 1939–1945 and *Day by Day with Bhagavan* 1945–1950. There are also reminiscences by devotees, edited by his great-nephew Sri V. Ganesan; the records of devotees in *The Power of the Presence*, three volumes, by David Godman, and *Living with Bhagavan*, a biography of Sri Annamalai Swami. Ramanashraman, presided over by the eldest great-nephew Sri S. Ramanam, has published over fifty-five books covering the written works and every aspect of Ramana

Maharshi's teaching and life. His recent biographer Sri Natarajan of Bangalore has also published numerous books and commentaries from his large Ramana Maharshi Centre for Learning.

It is generally accepted that Ramana Maharshi reserved his advanced teaching for close devotees whom he considered to be of sufficient maturity to absorb the full iconoclastic radicalism of Advaita Vedanta. With them he conversed and studied the uncompromising Advaita texts such as the *Rhibu Gita*, the *Ashtavakra Gita*, the *Avadhut Gita*, the *Yoga Vashista* and *Tripura Rhasa*, amongst others. His own *Forty Verses on Reality* gives his advanced teaching clearly and unequivocally, as do his essays on Self-enquiry, in the *Collected Works of Ramana Maharshi* published by Ramanashraman.

He translated, himself, the main texts of Shankara.* His teaching was essentially about Self-realization and he guided questioners to this ultimate understanding and its eventual attainment. Nevertheless out of infinite compassion for the questioners he never, ever destroyed their faith but made considerate concessions to their traditional Hindu beliefs, and then led them to the next step. His advanced teaching was reserved for the 'dry sticks', as David Godman points out in the standard work *Be As You Are*, and in his important anthology the answers are graded from the absolute level to the relative, concessionary plane.

Ramesh Balsekar takes up Ramana's teaching and enlightens questioners from the advanced, non-concessionary level of his Advaitic teaching. It is mainly the way of Surrender, with Self-enquiry as an addition. Spiritual practice is largely discarded, a preliminary focusing having been already practised and assumed to have happened by divine grace.

Ramesh has many edited books published by the Zen Chetana and Advaita Presses, recording his verbal teaching given at his flat in Mumbai. But unlike most other contemporary Advaita teachers he has actually written his own books. This anthology, approved by

---

* These, together with his *Forty Verses on Reality*, were published in one volume, *Ramana Shankara and the Forty Verses*, by Watkins Publishing in 2002.

Ramesh Balsekar and his leading disciple Wayne Liquorman, gives thematic extracts from all of the works written by him to date.

His aphorisms, edited by Gary Starbuck in *A Net of Jewels*, are extracts from written works and have not been included because I have tried to avoid too much repetition. Repetition is, however, a method widely used by Advaita teachers, including Ramesh, to hammer the pointers down, into the dense understanding of the wooden-headed pupil.

Ramesh has undoubtedly awakened many people to the ultimate understanding of Advaitic teaching. The most notable events where this has happened have been recorded in a book of tribute by pupils, *Like a Large Immovable Rock*, an appreciation of Ramesh Balsekar.

This remarkable man was educated at the London School of Economics and eventually, after a long career in banking, rose to become President of the Bank of India. At his retirement, after reading an article in *The Mountain Path* (the Ramanashramam Spiritual Bi-Monthly Review), he met the Mumbai sage, Nisargadatta Maharaj, author of *I Am That* (Chetana, Mumbai). He then began to translate the Maharaj's answers to seekers' questions, from Marathi into English, verbatim, as the Maharaj spoke. After doing this for three years he reached the ultimate understanding of Advaita and was twice given permission to teach by his Master. His early books are inspired by the Maharaj although Ramana Maharshi is quoted extensively. He is at the time of writing aged 84 but tirelessly gives dialogue seven days a week from his Mumbai penthouse.

I have added autobiographical notes in Ramesh's own words, culled from his books, as an appendix. He was influenced by the philosopher Wei Wu Wei (Terrence Gray), a prolific author, and also by the teachings of Chan Buddhism and Taoism. He has studied modern science, especially neurology and quantum physics, and has read Western and Indian philosophy extensively. His words speak for themselves, giving the quintessential Advaitic wisdom, all from his own experience.

Advaita is a growing movement, worldwide, and Ramesh, through his books and accessibility, has helped many seekers to end their intellectual doubts and proceed to an eventual understanding of the teaching – in other words, to wake up!

Shankara made the distinction between the *Para Vidya* (the esoteric high teaching) and the *Apara Vidya* (the lower exoteric teaching). Ramesh unmistakably, eloquently, without compromise gives the *Para Vidya*.

This book I trust will stimulate many readers to study the books he has written, his edited talks, and to meet him in Mumbai. I have endeavoured to give an overview of the salient points of his teaching leading to the Ultimate Understanding, the Self-realization as taught by Sri Ramana Maharshi, Maharaj Nisargadatta and now by Sri Ramesh S. Balsekar.

Alan Jacobs
London, 2002

PREFACE

A Poem of Creation

In its state of perfection, of total Awareness
IT is unaware of its awareness;
Then consciousness stirs into a moan of *Aum*,
and the dream-creation begins.
IT is conscious of *being*,
IT exults in this beingness,
Immersed in the love of *I-am-ness*,
IT expresses itself in duality.
Through union of twin aspects male-female,
Through the five elements —
Space-air-fire-water and earth,
Through the three Gunas —
Sattva-Rajas-Tamas —
IT manifests itself in duration.
In *dreamed* space-time
IT manifests as phenomena,
Creating millions of forms,
Breathing into them the life-force
And the all-pervading immanent consciousness;
Through these forms, in joyous self-love
functions consciousness as Prajna.
The sentient beings, mere images,
Thus conceived — wonder of wonders! —

Perceive one another as objects,

assuming subjectivity for oneself,

Each, in magnificent illusion,

Sees oneself as an entity separate,

With judgement and volition independent.

Each forgets his unlimited potential

as noumenal Absolute, accepts

His limited identity as an appearance,

A mere phenomenon;

Takes delivery of the functioning of Prajna

As his own personal actions,

Binds himself in illusory bondage,

And 'suffers' pain and pleasure!

Comes then, the merciful Guru,

Full of Grace and Light divine,

And shows him what it really is —

That which he thinks he is:

Nothing more than the speck of sperm

Impregnated in the mother's womb,

In which is latent the light of sentience

I-am-ness, the Consciousness that he is.

Given names in thousands,

Rama, Krishna, Ishwara, Brahman,

The same I-am-ness it is;

The light of Consciousness, Mahamaya,

In magnificent illusion, illudes

Its own nature and leads itself astray.

Until the Guru says: Halt, see yourself

As you are, in your true glory.

On your original state of timeless,

Absolute noumenality, has appeared

Like a temporary illness, the body-cum-consciousness,

Spontaneously, sans cause or reason,

as part of Prajnic functioning.

It works out its allotted duration

Until, just as spontaneously it disappears —

and consciousness, no longer conscious of itself,

Merges in Awareness — no one is born, no one dead.

In terms simple and direct:

What were you before you acquired the body?

Go back to the source; be still, and *then*

Will the seeker disappear and

Into the seeking merge.

No longer aware of awareness, in

Wholeness, in unicity, without duality *I am.*

With insight and intuition, with

deep conviction, simple to apprehend,

This-That-Is is beyond the bounds of intellect.

Only the objective and the phenomenal —

presence or absence — can the Intellect grasp.

But *what I Am* is neither presence nor absence;

Absence of the presence of presence,

Absence of the presence of absence,

Is *what I Am.*

POINTERS FROM NISARGADATTA MAHARAJ appendix iv

All these concepts have only one purpose: they are pointers to the Truth.

THE ULTIMATE UNDERSTANDING p. 20

I have said that there is writing but no author. Perhaps I should add that it is when the reader feels there is reading but no reader, that writing and reading would merge to produce apperception of the kind that never needs a comprehender.

EXPERIENCING THE TEACHING p. viii

Still, the question arises 'who' says so? 'Who' is writing this? No one, of course. There never has been a 'who' from the beginning of time, except *the 'Who' that is phenomenally ubiquitous and noumenally utterly absent!* The one who asks the question is the 'Who', that is the seeker, seeking Himself. It is not an individual speaking to another individual, but *Consciousness* speaking to Consciousness.

THE FINAL TRUTH p. 43

Ramesh S. Balsekar

ABSOLUTE

Shiva and Shakti are so intimately unified that they swallow each other all the time in order to prevent any breach in their unity; they separate themselves only to enjoy each other in their reciprocal love.

AMRITANUBHAVA BY JNANESHWAR

In this imagery, the poet-philosopher brings out in a unique way the closest possible relationship between the unicity of the unmanifest Absolute and the apparent duality of the manifested universe.

The sentient human being is only an infinitesimal part within the entire process of the mirrorization of the noumenon into the phenomenal universe. Therefore we (as human beings) cannot possibly have any essential nature of our own other than this *total* objectivization as such. At the same time, phenomena are not something separately created, or even projected independently, but are noumenon itself, conceptualized or objectivized. In other words, the difference between the two is purely notional – and this is the idea which is conveyed in this verse.

EXPERIENCE OF IMMORTALITY p. 6

The Absolute presence is eternally here and now. The Absolute presence can never forget itself, and the term 'remembering' is irrelevant; the sun never knows the night, so there is no question as to whether the sun knows the days!

RIPPLES p. 29

There can never be any 'experience' as such of the Absolute for the simple reason that there cannot possibly be anything objective about the Absolute, which is essentially pure subjectivity. It is the inner self-consciousness which is the experiencing medium for all experience. The Absolute provides the potentiality for the experience; the self provides the actuality.

The individual person's contact with the awareness of the Absolute can come about only when the mind is 'fasting' as it were, because then the process of conceptualizing ceases. When the mind is quiet, it reflects Reality; when the mind is absolutely motionless it dissolves and only Reality remains. That is why it is necessary to be one with consciousness. When the mind feasts, Reality disappears; when the mind fasts, Reality enters.

Awareness, when it is in contact with an object, a physical form, becomes witnessing. When at the same time there is self-identification with the object, such a state becomes 'the person'. In Reality, there is only one state; when corrupted and tainted by self-identification, it may be called a person (Vyakti); when it is tinted by a sense of being, the resulting consciousness becomes 'the witnessing'; when it remains in its pristine purity, untainted and untinted, it is the Supreme, the Absolute.

It is necessary to be clear about the difference, notional though it be, between awareness of the Absolute and the consciousness in which the universe appears. One is only the reflection of the other. But reflection of the sun in the dewdrop is not the sun. In the absence of objectivization, as in deep sleep, the apparent universe is not, but we are. This is so, because what we are is what the apparent universe is, and vice versa – dual in presence, non-dual in absence; irreconcilably separate in concept, inviolably united when unconceived.

POINTERS FROM NISARGADATTA MAHARAJ p. 11

ACCEPTANCE

At any moment, whatever is manifest is perfect. If this is deeply understood, every moment is welcomed and whatever that moment brings – 'good' or 'not good' – is accepted without any judgement, without expectation or anxiety. It is this attitude of acceptance which is the real freedom, freedom from expectation and desire, freedom from fear and anxiety. When this is deeply understood, you do not bother about what happens, what thoughts occur or what actions take place, or what emotions arise – they are all witnessed.

It will be found that the Guru and some of his disciples occasionally use the term 'God' as a synonym for the word 'Consciousness', with the subtle distinction usually lying in acceptance being felt and expressed as surrender to a Higher Power by those referring to God. And, clearly, in the ultimate understanding it is an *impersonal* Higher Power.

When the understanding is deep there is a feeling of gratitude and surrender to the Guru or Consciousness or Totality or God.

Such acceptance leads to accepting the body-mind organism as merely the instrument through which God or Consciousness as the SUBJECT expresses itself objectively.

Acceptance means just 'allowing' whatever is happening to happen:

Any event (including a thought) will be accepted without any judgement – and, quite importantly, even if a judgement or reaction did occur, no importance would be given to it. In other words, the events will be 'allowed' to occur without bothering about any allied aspects or consequences. Some thought arises, some action takes place. Egoic? Who cares?

CONSCIOUSNESS WRITES p. 11

All the items which make for 'insecurity' have existed since time immemorial – poverty, disease, death, war – and all along there have been a comparatively few persons of understanding who have accepted insecurity as an intrinsic part of what we call life. They have gained acceptance by using the understanding to take a qualitative jump from the relativity of involvement to the non-relativity of witnessing whatever happens as part of 'living'. Actually they have not *used* the understanding so much as that they have unconsciously *become* that understanding, that apperception that subjectivity is their real nature. They have accepted 'What-Is' at any moment as the objective expression of their subjective being. There is no question at all of any desire to change (through the supposed volition of the supposed individual) the 'What-Is' into something else. The basis of this understanding of their true nature is the conviction that the manifested universe (including the human being) is an illusion in consciousness, the appearance of which needs the concept of 'space' in which tri-dimensional objects could be presented and 'time' in which they could be observed. With this conviction, the human being with his intellect and volition and *pourasha** (and all the other concepts) is seen for the joke and the puppet that he is.

To put it simply, the essence of understanding is the acceptance – not the reluctant acceptance of frustration but the acceptance of utter conviction – of the fact that life, or living, is not a stagnant pool of water but a flowing river. It would be unhealthy to keep stagnant water for any length of time but you cannot keep *running* water in a bucket. If you would have running water, you must let it flow. The flow is the very nature of the river, and change is the very nature of life – and it must be accepted. Peace of mind, which is what most of humanity wants, consists not in grasping life in order to keep it secure for us, but in 'letting go'. It is rather ironic that the ultimate understanding comes not by holding on to the *concepts* of God but by letting go of all concepts concerning God. The ultimate understanding can come neither by straining to hang on to the material pleasures of the world nor by making efforts to seek and grasp the infinite absolute. It

* 'The Cosmic Spirit, the eternal and efficient cause of creation that gives conciousness to all manifestations.' From Glossary to *Pointers from Nisargadatta Maharaj.*

comes by accepting the finite and relative world of living, with all its limitations and its interrelated opposites, as the objective expression of our own subjective Self. The universe is the objective body of the subjective absolute.

THE FINAL TRUTH pp. 218 & 19

Acceptance as such, basically means accepting the characteristics of any given body-mind mechanism as part of the totality of phenomenal manifestation over which the concerned individual has no control. Such acceptance leads to:

    a) accepting one's own limitations not as something to improve upon with one's own efforts, but leaving the improvement, if any is needed, to the natural process. Such acceptance prevents any sense of frustration in case the efforts are not very successful;

    b) accepting the natural limitations of any 'other' body-mind mechanism without judgement (including the inability of that body-mind, at that moment, to 'accept');

    c) accepting, in any love/affection relationship, the prevailing relevant positive/negative or aggressive/passive roles according to the existing natural characteristics of the persons concerned in the relationship, irrespective of sex (male or female). Such acceptance of What-Is will prevent the arising of questions such as 'why should it be always me who has to give in?' Indeed, such genuine acceptance or understanding will almost certainly tend to produce a smoothening in the relationship. Any exceptionally difficult relationship will, of course, resolve itself one way or another in due course.

Acceptance, as such, also essentially means accepting the subjectivity of God or Totality or Consciousness or *Ishwara*, together with the existence of the 'me', the identification, as merely the operational element in the body-mind organism. Such acceptance leads to:

    a) accepting the body-mind organism as merely the instrument through which God or Consciousness as the Subject expresses itself objectively;

5

b) attention being paid wholly to the work in hand, without its being spread to the periphery through worries about the results or consequences; this obviously leads to a conservation of energy that would otherwise have been wasted in the form of tension and stress;

c) a combination of tolerance and humility which becomes utterly irresistible in human relationships. When there is acceptance about one's own limitations, there arises a natural tolerance about the limitations in 'others'. The resulting humility is not the interconnected opposite of 'pride'; we often find that the supposedly 'humble' people are some of the proudest people we know, the apparent humility being the cloak of hypocrisy. The true humility is the natural consequence of the surrender of the 'me' as the do-er, always in competition with the rest of the world.

Acceptance/understanding very often makes the relevant body-mind mechanism extremely sensitive, and to that extent the mirrored suffering or pleasure becomes more intense: the *jnani* weeps with those who weep and laughs with those who laugh, without any sense of personal embarrassment in either case.

CONSCIOUSNESS TO CONSCIOUSNESS p. 68

ACTION

This provides the answer to the usual objection raised against the injunction to act without expecting and wanting the fruits of action – that such an injunction will lead to 'fatalistic' attitude, i.e. a person will have no reason to act at all, and he would therefore be inclined not to act at all. In other words, you may want to desist from action if you cannot have the fruits of your action. But the fact of the matter is that the fruits of the action will depend on the destiny of the organism, whereas the energy within the body-mind organism will continue to produce activity in accordance with the natural characteristics with which the organism was conceived and created. These natural characteristics depend on the genes – the DNA – of the organism and the conditioning that the organism has received from the environment in which it was raised. And the essential fact is that no one has the control either over the DNA or over the environment in which the organism was born; no one can choose one's parents and, by the same token, no one can choose the environment in which one is born, and gets conditioned in.

To one who has transcended his ego, the routine work during the day is no longer required as self-discipline but is a natural fulfillment of his Self-realization. Such a man of Wisdom does not need to work in order to get his material requirements which go on increasing continuously for the ordinary man. He is perfectly content in the very Divine Nature – that provides eternal satisfaction for him. Where contentment has finally arrived in the very Self-realization, desires cannot arise, and in the absence of involvement in the desires there is no question of any action to satisfy the desires; nor are there any obligatory duties for such a Self-realized man because such duties concern only the man who has desires. Whatever work such a man does, just happens without any trace of doership.

Such a Self-realized man, rooted in the experience of the Self, does not have to depend for his satisfaction on any object or person because he is centered in the eternal subject.

What an ordinary person considers 'his' actions, are really reactions produced by the brain in response to the senses when they meet their respective objects. Thus when the eyes see something or the ears hear something, the brain reacts to this event according to the natural characteristics of the body-mind organism, and produces a reaction. It is this natural reaction to the event which the ordinary man mistakenly considers his action.

The wise man, *Tattvavith* – who knows Reality – on the other hand, understands what really happens and does not involve himself with whatever happens. In other terms, the wise man considers all events as God's actions and therefore does not judge them as 'good' or 'bad'.

Ramakrishna Paramahaunsa gave his disciples this simple advice: 'Be absolutely convinced that you are merely a machine which is operated upon by God, and then you may do whatever you want.'

THE BHAGAVAD GITA ch. 18 vv. 35–42

If there is no lock, what is the use of the master key? How does the master key work? If nothing really has happened and the phenomenal manifestation is merely a mirage or a sound that has appeared and would finally merge in its source, how is one to live one's normal life? Life is like a dream, like a stage play where the various actors play their respective roles while never really being unaware of their true identity. The expert actor playing the role of a king is never for a moment unaware of the fact that he is really a pauper; he *lives* the role of a king and never while acting does he *think* of the hardships of being a pauper. In life, thus, what we are expected to do is to live our roles naturally and accept whatever life brings in its course according to the grand design of the totality of phenomenal functioning. All that one is expected to do – and indeed all that one can do – is to live according to the inherent nature of the psychosomatic apparatus, and let the deep understanding of our true nature work such changes as are considered necessary, without any thinking or volition on our part. Any attempt at controlling our inherent nature can only result in suppression and its adverse consequences. All that is necessary is the witnessing of whatever happens in life, including the thoughts and acts of the 'me' while being *passively but continuously* aware of our true identity (such awareness is indeed the true understanding). Then, there is no wanting to change the 'what is' to what the 'me' thinks 'what-should-be' because the understanding comports the realization that all the 'me's' concerned in life are *together* truly the eternal, subjective 'I' expressing itself objectively as the phenomenal manifestation in its totality.

EXPLORATIONS INTO THE ETERNAL p. iv

We seem to have arrived at a working formula on the subject. *What is the individual to do?* The only thing one can do is always to keep in mind the fact that an independent entity cannot exist, and also the fact that the entire manifestation is the functioning of consciousness in which each one of us has one's allotted role to play and, finally, to accept whatever happens within that total functioning with a sense of wondrous admiration. The one thing that remains thereafter is not any 'practicing' as a deliberate effort, but merely to let our true understanding deeply impregnate our very being, passively and patiently, so that all illusions and obstructions gradually fall off by themselves.

POINTERS FROM NISARGADATTA MAHARAJ p. 211

ADVAITA

The question that would arise at this early stage is: if the basic premise of Advaita Vedanta is that nothing has happened and that the Absolute is pure awareness not aware of its existence, then how does one account for this manifested universe which is very much there to be experienced by all?

The answer is that what is manifested is merely an appearance in consciousness that is experienced through MAYA. And Maya is a concept which is brought in only to prove the main premise of the unicity of the Absolute, which is pure subjectivity without the slightest touch of any objectivity or duality. The concept of Maya is like the concept of 'x' in algebra which is introduced merely to arrive at the answer, and is rejected as without substance once the answer has been arrived at. If one at any time ignores the fact that Maya is merely a concept, a supposed quantity 'x', one gets involved in all kinds of avoidable, imagined difficulties.

EXPERIENCE OF IMMORTALITY pp. 1–2

The knowledge of the Self is Advaita, that is non-duality, but it is to be acquired in apparent duality so that the duality disappears in due course when one remains firmly in that knowledge. Instead of looking ahead as one usually does, one must look back and seek the source in order to realize one's true beingness. ('Looking back' is to be interpreted in the sense that the eye can see the objects in front of it but it cannot see itself; if one wants to see one's own eyes, it can be done only by the mind, the mind can be seen only through intellect, and it is consciousness which can witness the intellect.)

EXPLORATIONS INTO THE ETERNAL p. 42

The quantum theory clearly suggests a connection between every particle in the universe, and the formulation of the physicist J.S. Bell, known as Bell's Theorem, particularly brings out the fact that spatially separated events cannot be considered as independent happenings, and that their significance lies in the interconnectedness of events *apparently removed in distance* in a manner that cannot be either understood or explained by man's ordinary experience. This suggestion brings the working of the universe startlingly close to the Eastern mystic's intuitive view of the universe as a net of jewels – Indra's net – in which each of the millions of jewels reflects all other jewels.

EXPLORATIONS INTO THE ETERNAL p. iii

APPERCEPTION*

The master key to all doors of ignorance and confusion is the apperception ('mind's perception of itself' – *The Concise Oxford Dictionary*) that nothing in relativity exists, not even knowledge. There is no creation, no dissolution.

THE ULTIMATE UNDERSTANDING p. 8

Apperception brings about the cessation of desire, positive or negative – that is to say, the cessation of the desire to accept and the cessation of the desire to reject – the desire to accept the acceptable and the desire to reject the unacceptable; the desire to accept what people will applaud and the desire to reject what people might condemn. When there is apperception, there is the clear understanding that it is the energy of the consciousness which experiences all experience.

THE FINAL TRUTH p. 181

With the apperception comes the conviction – or with the conviction comes the apperception – that the distinction between the universal Consciousness and the personal consciousness was only notional. It was like the distinction between the wave and the water in the wave, or between the word and that to which it refers.

A breeze flowing through certain flowers passes on their fragrance, so also Consciousness creates bodies appropriate to the notions with which it entertains and identifies itself. Through these bodies, which it energizes, it then experiences the consequences of those notions.

THE FINAL TRUTH p. 231

* A term that was coined by Leibnitz in his *New Essays* (1696), widely used by Immanuel Kant and Terrence Gray (Wei Wu Wei). [Ed.]

ART

In Indian music, especially classical and semi-classical music, there is an unusual tradition that the members of the audience are free to vocally express their appreciation while the performance goes on. As happens everywhere, there are hypocrites, bent on impressing other people, who do not really understand the nuances of great music but add their own contributions to those of the genuine ones.

An emperor in India, himself a great musician, was much irked by such hypocrites, and decided to do something about it. On a ceremonial occasion, when he himself was to give a performance, he suddenly announced that anyone who interrupted his performance would be put to death. There was a stunned silence. The performance began, the silence continued, until it was suddenly broken by one spontaneous burst of appreciation from the audience. The emperor stopped singing, the terrified culprit was brought before the emperor. The emperor glared at the culprit and stood up to face him. Then suddenly with a big smile, the emperor embraced him and rewarded him with one of the necklaces from around his own neck.

It is this same intuitive spontaneity which makes a Sufi run out on the streets shouting 'I am God,' or makes a student of Advaita suddenly burst out in an uncontrollable fit of crying or laughter.

THE ULTIMATE UNDERSTANDING pp. 184–5

When such an exchange of dialogue between the guru and the Self-realized disciple (a spontaneous outpouring) is viewed purely from the intellectual point of view, it would be seen as unnecessary repetition. But from the viewpoint of a sincere seeker it would bring tears of joy, as would a piece of classical music expertly rendered by a musical maestro, however often the aficionado might have heard it before. To the music lover each rendering brings out something unique, something he has never felt before. There is no need to compare and judge. If you sit on the shore of the ocean and watch the waves keep rolling in, you can keep on watching the sight, and then you will realize that while they are all waves, each has some distinct personality, that in the unicity there is a beautiful diversity in phenomenality which is most wondrous to behold.

A DUET OF ONE p. 95

When there is apperception of the totality of What-Is, the meaning of life becomes very clear: life is just a dance, the purpose and meaning of which is only to dance, and when the dance is over, you are precisely where you were – on the floor. When you dance, there is no expectation of anything to achieve. Before you started to dance, you were still and then there was movement when the dance began, and when the dance ended, there was again stillness.

THE FINAL TRUTH p. 62

The entire manifested creation presents a cosmic dance by the divine dancer, and *the dance cannot be differentiated from the dancer.* The dance is executed to the tune of time or duration, and takes place on the stage of space. The various movements are the various aspects and potencies. It is the potency of the natural order of events and sequences which presents the theme of the dance based on the specific characteristics of each object (from a blade of grass to the conceptual creator Brahma), reacting to the various events and sequences. The natural order (*the niyati*) is the dancer presenting the dance drama of phenomenal manifestation and its functioning. It is Consciousness which has spontaneously, causelessly, been stirred out of its state of rest into one of movement, by the cosmic thought 'I Am'. The dance exhibits various epochs and seasons and portrays moods of every conceivable nature, like love and hate, compassion and anger, etc. It is set against the background music of the elements, on a stage illuminated by the sun and the moon and the stars, with the *dramatis personae* provided by all the sentient beings in the entire universe.

The infinite Consciousness though not different from its aspect as the dancer (natural order) and the dance itself, is the silent but alert witness – *drashta* – of this cosmic dance drama happening *within* itself.

THE FINAL TRUTH p. 20

Is it not possible, if you are interested in music, to listen to a performance without the intrusion of the individual listener – when the music and the listening are without any separation?

EXPERIENCING THE TEACHING p. 62

As regards the arts, the Zen artists – both poets and painters – have as their favorite subjects what might be called natural, specific and secular things. Not only are the subjects natural but the techniques themselves are natural, involving what is known as the art of artlessness or what Sabro Hasegawa has called the 'controlled accident' – neither the purely convergent nor the wholly divergent elements but a natural balance between the two. The essential point is that there is no dichotomy, and the total operation of the intellect is considered as natural as the formative behaviour of plants or birds. In other words, there is a beautiful natural blending of discipline and spontaneity – discipline being not constructive and spontaneity being not licentious. It is in this insight that opposites are interrelated and necessary for the existence of each other in a vivacious balance which avoids conflict. This insight also makes it clear that where a conflict does arise, it is superficial and easily rectified when it is seen in its true colours. Thus for instance, a most striking feature of the Sung landscape – as in most of sumi-e type of painting – is the relative emptiness of the picture which is not just the unpainted part of the material; indeed it is the apparent emptiness which gives the picture its very life and soul. The secret of this type of painting – that is in fact painting by restraining oneself from painting, or 'playing the stringless lute' – is of course, balancing form and emptiness, balancing the manifested actual and the unmanifested potential, balancing the natural silence with the spoken word, and thus suggesting the limitless potential of the void from which suddenly arises the phenomenal manifestation. A stranger to this type of painting at once notices an absence of the regularity and symmetry that characterizes convergent thinking and which is almost predictable; instead he sees something apparently eccentric and shapeless, and yet uncommonly well balanced, throbbing with vitality.

EXPLORATIONS INTO THE ETERNAL p. 102

AWAKENING

S hen Hui says: 'There is a difference between awakening and
deliverance: the former is sudden, thereafter deliverance is gradual ...
In fact what we mean by "sudden enlightenment" is the perfect equiv-
alence of phenomenal understanding with the universal principal:
this is not reached by any stages at all.'

This is perhaps one of the clearest, most authoritative and unam-
biguous statements any master has left. What sudden enlightenment
indicates is the mending of the dichotomy of the whole-mind whereby
the operation of the split-mind no longer prevails.

EXPERIENCE OF IMMORTALITY pp. 234–5

BIOGRAPHY

This is the background of the *Experience of Immortality*. The title of the book, as Jnaneshwar himself states in the text, is Anubhava-Amrita, but at some juncture it got converted to *Amritanubhava* (the meaning in both cases would remain the same – experience of immortality), perhaps because it was slightly easier to pronounce that way.

I do hope that the reader will admire this book and learn from it as much as I did in writing it. And then, of course, there is the promise by Jnaneshwar that those who have apprehended the integral message of *Anubhava-Amrita* will themselves become merged in that experience (of immortality). Relatively speaking, if I have been of some little assistance to the reader in apprehending this integral message, I shall have repaid my debts to both Sage Jnaneshwar and to my Sadguru Nisargadatta Maharaj. Ultimately, of course, the fact remains that there are only books not authors, only writing not writers.

EXPERIENCE OF IMMORTALITY pp. ii–iii

BONDAGE

The question of 'bondage' and 'freedom' can arise only if the true nature of the 'individual' has not been well and truly understood. When there is a clear realization of the fundamental fact that the individual is the manifest appearance of the unmanifest, the question of bondage cannot arise. The question cannot arise for the simple reason that the questioner does not truly exist except as an appearance in Consciousness, a movement in the mind.

Bondage for the supposed individual appears because of a mistaken identity. What-We-Are is the animating Consciousness – which is noumenon. What we *think* we are is the phenomenal object to which the animating Consciousness provides sentience. The only 'existence' any phenomenal object, including the human being, can have is merely apparent. That is to say, it is only an appearance in Consciousness, an objectivization that is entirely dependent for its existence on the mind that objectivizes it. In other words, the existence of the phenomenal object, with mind as its only nature (like any dreamed character), cannot possibly have any independent nature of its own.

THE FINAL TRUTH pp. 48 & 50

BRAIN

It is clear that the brain, with its fantastic memory bank, is an absolute necessity in order to live in this world. But the trouble is that the individual mind is a split or divided mind and we cannot ignore the whole mind because the whole mind is the *basic* universal Consciousness. Indeed, most physical processes concerning breathing, swallowing, digesting, circulating of blood, etc. are extraordinarily complex processes with which the brain has little to do. These processes are called 'involuntary' and brushed aside as of little consequence. This is where the root of the whole trouble lies – the dichotomy created in the modern man between his brain (the cortex) and the rest of his body, between the whole mind and the split-mind, between the 'I' and 'me', between the impersonal or universal Consciousness and the personal consciousness identified with the separate psychosomatic apparatus. In other words, we need both the brain-thinking and the instinctive wisdom to lead a harmonious and well-balanced life, but what we have done is to allow the brain thinking to develop so quickly and so fast that we have almost forgotten all about the instinctive wisdom which has thereby nearly slumped into atrophy.

THE FINAL TRUTH p. 155

CONSCIOUSNESS

Shiva and Shakti belong together, have the same inherent nature, and have lived happily together from time immemorial, undivided in their duality.

Jnaneshwar brings out in this verse the important point that awareness and consciousness (or, consciousness-at-rest and consciousness-in-movement) are separate only as a concept – the division is purely notional – and that they are inviolably united when unconceived; that they are dual only in presence since the concept of time came into being, and non-dual in absence when time was not conceived. He avers this again as a reminder because in the previous verse he had said that the manifestation of the universe does not take place as a third thing apart from consciousness-at-rest and consciousness-in-movement. That the separateness is purely notional is stressed here by referring to the essential unity in the absence of any concept of time and the associated sense of presence.

EXPERIENCE OF IMMORTALITY p. 12

Consciousness is the only 'capital' that a sentient being is born with. This is the apparent position. The real situation, however, is that what is born is consciousness, which needs an organism to manifest itself in, and that organism is the physical body.

What is it that gives sentience – capacity to feel sensations, to respond to stimuli – to a sentient being? What is it that distinguishes a person who is alive from the one who is dead? It is, of course, the *sense of being*, the knowledge of being present, consciousness, the 'activizing' spirit which animates the physical construct of the body.

It is consciousness indeed that manifests itself in individual forms and gives them apparent existence. In human beings through such manifestation arises the concept of a separate 'I'. In each individual the Absolute gets reflected as awareness, and thus pure Awareness becomes self-awareness, or consciousness.

What is the actual substance of this animating consciousness? Obviously, it must be physical material because in the absence of the physical form it cannot survive. Manifested consciousness can exist only as long as its abode, the body, is kept in a sound and habitable condition. Although consciousness is a reflection of the Absolute, it is time-bound and can be sustained only by the food material, comprising the five elements, that the physical body is. Consciousness resides in a healthy body and abandons it when it is decayed and moribund. Reflection of the sun can be seen only in a clear dewdrop, not in a muddy one.

We are so accustomed to thinking of ourselves as bodies having consciousness, that we find it very difficult to accept or even understand the real position. Actually it is consciousness which manifests itself in innumerable bodies. It is, therefore, essential to apperceive that birth and death are nothing but the beginning and the ending of a stream of movements in consciousness, interpreted as events in space-time. If we can realize this, we shall also realize that we are pure being-awareness-bliss in our original pristine state, and when in touch with consciousness, we are only the witnessing of (and totally apart from) the various movements in consciousness. This is an indisputable fact, because obviously, *we cannot be what we perceive; the perceiver must be different from what he perceives.*

The entire manifested universe exists only in consciousness. The conceptualized process would be as follows: Consciousness arises in Pure Being, for no particular cause or reason other than that it is its nature to do so – like waves on the surface of the sea. In consciousness the world appears and disappears; and each one of us is entitled to say: 'All there is, is I, all there is, is mine; before all beginnings, after all endings, I am there to witness whatever happens.' 'Me', 'you' and 'he' are only *appearances in consciousness – all are basically 'I'.*

It is not that the world does not exist. As an appearance in consciousness, the world is the totality of the known in the potential of the unknown. *The world can be said to appear, but not be.* Duration of the appearances, of course, will differ according to the different scales of time. Apart from the fact that the world disappears in deep sleep and re-appears in the waking state, the duration of its appearance would vary according to the allotted span of one's life-time – a few hours for an insect and aeons for the trinity of Brahma, Vishnu and Maheshwara! Ultimately, however, whatever is an appearance in consciousness must end, and it cannot have any reality.

It is necessary to be clear about the difference, notional though it be, between awareness of the Absolute and the consciousness in which the universe appears, Maharaj repeatedly warns us. One is only the reflection of the other. But reflection of the sun in the dewdrop is not the sun. In the absence of objectivization, as in deep sleep, the apparent universe is not, but we are. This is so, because what we are is what the apparent universe is, and vice versa – dual in presence, non-dual in absence; irreconcilably separate in concept, inviolably united when unconceived.

POINTERS FROM NISARGADATTA MAHARAJ pp. 3–11

The knowledge *I am* or consciousness is the only 'capital' a sentient being has. Indeed, without consciousness he would not have any sentience.

When this *I-am-ness* is not present, as in deep sleep, there is no body, no outside world, and no 'God'. It is evident that a tiny speck of this consciousness contains the entire universe.

Nevertheless, consciousness cannot exist without a physical body, and existence of the body being temporal, consciousness also must be temporal.

Finally, if consciousness is time-bound and is not eternal, any knowledge that is acquired through the medium of consciousness cannot be the truth and is, therefore, ultimately to be rejected, or, as I said, to be offered to Brahman as an oblation – Brahman being consciousness, beingness, I-am-ness, or Ishwara, or God, or whatever name you give it. In other words, the interrelated opposites, both knowledge and ignorance, are in the area of the known and, therefore, not the truth – and truth is only in the unknown. Once this is clearly understood, nothing more remains to be done. Indeed there is really no 'entity' to do anything.

POINTERS FROM NISARGADATTA MAHARAJ p. 38

Consciousness has fallaciously identified itself with the individual psychosomatic apparatus as the 'me', so is constantly seeking its own source. And the joke is that all there is, is consciousness; therefore, what consciousness is seeking as its source is itself! The search goes on until there is apperception that consciousness is the 'I' awareness that cannot be aware of itself because awareness knows no self of which it could be aware. Divided and split into cognizing subject/cognized objects, 'I' cognizes every conceptual thing that can be cognized except that which is cognizing. That which is cognizing is not conceivable since it is no thing; and it is no thing since it is not conceivable!

EXPERIENCING THE TEACHING p. 87

It is consciousness alone which is our constant companion, and it is the continuous attention to one's stream of consciousness that takes one on to Awareness – the basic existence, that-which-is-life-love-joy. The very consciousness of being conscious is already a movement towards Awareness. The mind by its very nature is out-going, always tending to seek the source of things within the things themselves. When it is directed towards the source within, it is almost like the beginning of a new life. Awareness replaces consciousness. The 'I am', which is a thought in consciousness, ceases. In awareness, there is no thought. Awareness is the source of consciousness.

POINTERS FROM NISARGADATTA MAHARAJ p. 13

All that exists is universal Consciousness. The universe *as such* is not the universal Consciousness, but Consciousness *is* the universe, just as the bracelet is made of gold but the gold is not made of the bracelet.

CONSCIOUSNESS AND MANIFESTATION
EXPERIENCING THE TEACHING p. xii

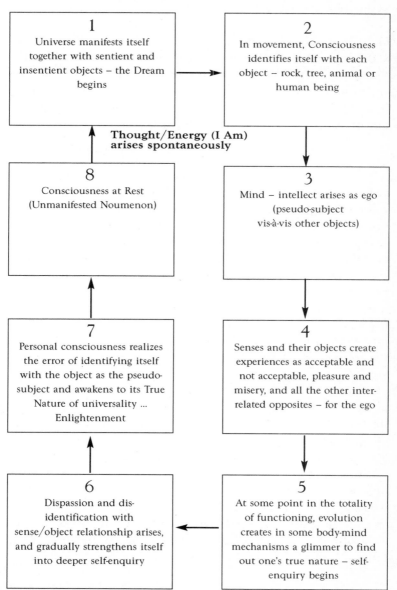

1

Universe manifests itself together with sentient and insentient objects – the Dream begins

2

In movement, Consciousness identifies itself with each object – rock, tree, animal or human being

Thought/Energy (I Am) arises spontaneously

8

Consciousness at Rest (Unmanifested Noumenon)

3

Mind – intellect arises as ego (pseudo-subject vis-à-vis other objects)

7

Personal consciousness realizes the error of identifying itself with the object as the pseudo-subject and awakens to its True Nature of universality ... Enlightenment

4

Senses and their objects create experiences as acceptable and not acceptable, pleasure and misery, and all the other inter-related opposites – for the ego

6

Dispassion and dis-identification with sense/object relationship arises, and gradually strengthens itself into deeper self-enquiry

5

At some point in the totality of functioning, evolution creates in some body-mind mechanisms a glimmer to find out one's true nature – self-enquiry begins

Whether the manifested universe exists or not, Consciousness is there as the subjective Absolute.

Millions of universes appear in the infinite Consciousness (the *Chitakasha*), forming a totality of the known form (the *Mahad-akasha*) in the totality of the formless unknown. These millions of universes appear in the infinite Consciousness like specks of dust, illuminated by a beam of light. Each individual universe merely reflects the illumination, it is certainly not the cause.

THE FINAL TRUTH pp. 16–17

Consciousness is the fragrance in the flower! Just as a forest conflagration, though itself a single body of flame, assumes many forms, so does the formless, non-dual Consciousness assume various forms as objects in the universe. Consciousness is the subtle solution of continuity in the innumerable universes which are forever potentially present in it, precisely as the flavor of the foodstuffs is potentially present in the ingredients but is made manifest by cooking them. All universes would instantly collapse like a house of cards if Consciousness were not. All concepts of pleasure and misery collapse in the presence of Consciousness, precisely like darkness collapses in the presence of light.

The totality of creation is in the heart of the infinite Consciousness, just as one's personal dream is in one's mind, both as the cause and the effect. I-am-ness is itself conceptual 'creation'. The interdependent opposites like virtue and sin, good and evil, positive and negative, subject and object, which create the separation that is the source of all suffering, are mere notions without any basis of reality. They have no independent existence. It is only the one pure infinite Consciousness which appears as diverse objects in a dream. These dream-objects disappear in deep sleep, precisely as this apparently real dream-world, which appears in our apparent waking-state, disappears in the cosmic dissolution which is the equivalent of the deep sleep state.

THE FINAL TRUTH pp. 25–7

DEATH

It is necessary to make a distinction – perhaps subtle but very necessary – between mourning for someone and reacting emotionally to the loss of a near relative or a dear friend. It is natural for the body-mind organism to react to the loss of someone who has been close to one, especially over a long period. While such a spontaneous reaction is perfectly natural, prolonged mourning or grieving over a period is a matter of involvement of the ego through identification with the body. In other words, while an emotional reaction is perfectly natural, an involvement is a matter of ignorance.

Ramana Maharshi was once greatly upset emotionally when a companion over a long period suddenly died. As an explanation he came out with a very similar view.

Man is not prepared to give up the relative 'me' so as to be the absolute 'I'. He wants the 'me', a phenomenal object, to become the absolute subject. It is like the case of a drowning man who is not prepared to let go of his heavy hoard of gold. Man is not prepared to accept death as the final disintegration of the object 'me' so that he could be the eternal and only subject 'I' – he wants and expects death as a temporary disintegration that would bring for the 'me' unalloyed and perpetual joy and happiness.

When a man witnesses the death of another, what he sees is that the organism stops functioning, and because his intellect tells him – and his deep-rooted intuition convinces him – he *knows* that it is the body that is dead and that he himself – the one who was there a hundred years ago and who will be there a hundred years hence – cannot die. He also knows that this one who survives the physical death does not have the form that he had when he lived. But he cannot envisage the possibility that THAT *which has always been eternally present does not need a form* in order to be present – visible or invisible, material or immaterial – because he cannot give up the idea of a separate entity as a 'me'.

Man finds it extraordinarily difficult to accept the total annihilation of the phenomenal object with which there is identification as a separate entity. Such identification persists beyond his concept of the death of the physical apparatus, expecting the 'me' to exist in some other world. In other words, he cannot give up the idea of space-time representation for the 'me', and he asks where does one go after death? The problem and mystery of death is thus based firmly on the concept of a 'me' (as opposed to the 'other' or 'not-me') who will some time or the other reach the point of departure called 'death' which is known, and who will presumably go to a destination *in space-time* which is not known. In point of fact, death poses a problem which is not truly a problem at all because this problem is based on false and illusory conceptualization. There is truly no 'me' at all to go anywhere. A deep understanding of this fact alone, as Maharaj used to say, would constitute enlightenment.

Two incidents concerning the Chinese sage Chuang-Tzu would put the matter in perspective:

  i) A friend of the sage went to visit him in order to offer his condolences on the death of his wife, and found him sitting with his legs spread out, pounding on an inverted tub and singing lustily. When he expressed his displeasure at this unseemly conduct, Chuang-Tzu said, 'When my wife died, do you think I did not grieve like anyone else? Then I looked back to her beginning and the time before she was born; not only before she was born, but the time before she had a body, not only the time before she had a body, but the time before she had a spirit. In the midst of the confused jumble of mystery and wonder there was a change and she had a spirit; a second change and she had a body; another change and she was born. Now there has been a further change and she is dead. It is exactly like the progression of the seasons – spring, summer, autumn, winter.'

ii) Writing on the death of his Master, Lao-Tzu, Chuang-Tzu says: 'The Master came because it was time for him to come. He left because he followed the natural flow of events. Be content with each moment of eternity and be willing to follow the flow. Then there will be no cause for joy or grief. In the old days this was called freedom from bondage. The wood is consumed but the fire burns on, and we do not know when it will come to an end.'

Near-death experiences can happen only to the ego, and it just cannot be denied that the ego has no real existence; the ego is purely a concept, an illusion, and it is only when the ego is totally annihilated that real beingness comes into being. BEING is cognized as 'That' which, by its very nature, can never be non-being.

Man wants to know the meaning and significance of life and death. The beautiful flower that blooms in the wilderness for a brief period of time is as much a part of the manifested universe as is man. The flower is not concerned with the meaning of its existence, nor is the wild beast in the jungle worried about the meaning of life and death, although it is as much a sentient being as is man. Meaning is clearly not something connected with things themselves; it is a function of the mind, of the intellect, and therefore different persons find different meanings in the same things.

What happens after death? We would obviously be in the same state that we were in before life started in the womb; we would return to the source, the perennial potential. Nature would proceed in any case along its normal course, but, if intellect is prevented from conceptualizing and thus interfering with the natural fluidity of the mind, we would be freed from the unnecessary harrowing anticipations. It is possible, therefore, to erase the horror of death from consciousness, but it would be almost impossible to do so deliberately and purposefully because the mind (which is the content of consciousness) is notoriously persistent about something which it is asked to avoid.

EXPLORATIONS INTO THE ETERNAL pp. 180–98

DESIRE

Ashtavakra warns his disciple that desire will destroy itself gradually, but only when its power of destruction is constantly borne in mind. By this he suggests that no positive action like suppressing desire could ever achieve any success in destroying desire. On the contrary, any positive action will only strengthen desire. The only way to destroy desire is to witness passively the arising of desire each time it happens, without any involvement. Such witnessing will cut off vertically any horizontal extension of the desire which involvement clearly indicates. Even the active quest for knowledge could be considered a positive action. Ashtavakra assures Janaka that he is the pure Consciousness whereas all else is illusory, including ignorance. Wherefore, he asks, the quest for knowledge?! Why, too, the need for doing good deeds, the basis of which is again a desire for something in return? Finally, he reminds the disciple about all the positive efforts that he has put in, life after life, for the acquisition of knowledge and enlightenment. All these efforts have been an exercise in futility. At least now, he appeals to his disciple, stop all positive effort and *just be.*

A DUET OF ONE p. 79

The desires that arise in a state of liberation are in the course of the natural functions and are devoid of any craving for external objects. Such basic desires that existed even prior to contact with sense objects continue to exist. They are natural, spontaneous, not based on thought and therefore free of the impurity of dualism. Truth is non-dual, but all action necessarily involves duality because all functioning can only take place in apparent duality. Indeed, apperception comports the understanding that any difference between duality and non-duality is purely conceptual. Duality and non-duality are a pair of interrelated opposites, like innumerable other such polarities without which manifestation could not take place. When all concepts cease, when conceptualization itself ceases, what remains is the unicity of the Absolute.

THE FINAL TRUTH p. 233

All desire means movement in consciousness, which is conceptualizing and therefore bondage. Desire includes even the desire for liberation! This is so because it can only be the ego which desires anything, including liberation. Awareness and apperception of this fact destroys the ego, and then enlightenment is apperceived as not a personal event but a happening in totality. Who is bound by whom – and who is liberated by whom?!

THE FINAL TRUTH p. 182

DEVOTION

At the end of the talk, each day, bhajans were sung, and then the singer would bow down and touch the feet of the Guru. Some of the visitors would follow, and in the meantime I would keep my palms joined in a namaste, with my eyes closed; afterwards, I would leave the room.

When I myself used to bend down on my knees at the feet of my own Guru, I had the clearest understanding that I myself was bending down before my Guru's Self, and that my Self and my Guru's Self was, indeed, the One Self, Consciousness, pure Subjectivity.

THE ULTIMATE UNDERSTANDING p. 259

Now then, what exactly is this 'God'? Is he not the very consciousness – the sense of 'being' that one has – because of which you are able to ask questions? 'I am' itself is God. What is it that you love most? Is it not this 'I am', the conscious presence which you want to preserve at any cost? The seeking itself is God. In seeking you discover that 'you' are apart from this body-mind complex. If you were not conscious, would the world exist for you? Would there be any idea of a God? And, the consciousness in you and the consciousness in me – are they different? Are they not separate only as concepts, seeking unity unconceived, and is that not love?

POINTERS FROM NISARGADATTA MAHARAJ p. 33

The moment the false identity is liquidated, there is nothing left to identify with, except the totality! And this is the experience of the Jnani, the *Bhakta*, as well as the Yogi.

Maharaj hits the nail on the head in regard to this subject of devotion and knowledge when he says that the two are so inextricably blended together that they are in effect one and the same thing: love

for self and love for God are not different. The following words,
reproduced from *I Am That,* * are truly illuminating:

> That which you are, your true self, you love it, and
> whatever you do, you do for your own happiness.
> To find it, to know it, to cherish it is your basic urge.
> Since time immemorial you loved yourself, but not
> wisely. Use your body and mind wisely in the service
> of the self, that is all. Be true to your own self, love
> your self absolutely. Do not pretend that you love
> others as yourself. Unless you have realized them as
> one with yourself, you cannot love them. Don't
> pretend to be what you are not, don't refuse to be
> what you are. Your love of others is the result of self-
> knowledge, not its cause. Without Self-realization, no
> virtue is genuine. When you know beyond all
> doubting that the same life flows through all that is,
> and you are that life, you will love all naturally and
> spontaneously. When you realize the depth and
> fullness of your love for yourself, you know that every
> living being and the entire universe are included in
> your affection. But when you look at anything as
> separate from you, you cannot love it for you are
> afraid of it. Alienation causes fear and fear deepens
> alienation. It is a vicious circle. Only Self-realization
> can break it. Go for it resolutely.

The problem which Maharaj has set out so pointedly – that you
cannot love anything which you consider as separate from you because
then you are afraid of it, and the more you try the more difficult it
becomes – is a type of problem which modern psychiatric anthro-
pologists call the 'double-bind' type, where a person is required to do
something contradictory. For example, the more you are asked to relax
the more tense you become; the longer you want to hit the golf ball
the more tense you become and the shorter the distance the ball
travels!

* Chetana Publishers, Mumbai, rev. ed., ch. 46, p. 213.

Without Self-realization no virtue is genuine; it is only when you arrive at the deepest conviction that the same life flows through everything, and that you are that life, that you begin to love all naturally and spontaneously. Such conviction, of course, can only come through an intuitive apperception, and Nature (*Nisarga*) will have its own course for this intuitive process.

In regard to the identity of the self and God, it is interesting to note the very close similarity of teaching between the great mystics of various faiths in different ages. We are told by St. John of the Cross, in his Canticles, that 'The thread of love binds so closely God and the soul, and so unites them, that it transforms them and makes them one by love; so that, though in essence different yet in glory and appearance the soul seems God, and God the soul.' (Canticles XXXI). And further: 'Let me be so transformed in Thy beauty, that, being alike in beauty, we may see ourselves both in Thy beauty; so that one beholding the other, each may see his own beauty in the other, the beauty of both being Thine only, and mine absorbed in it.' (Canticles XXXVI). Also the great Plotinus tells us: 'If then a man sees himself become one with the One, he has in himself likeness of the One.' (Enneads VI. 9.9.11).

POINTERS FROM NISARGADATTA MAHARAJ pp. 204–6

The external worship of a form as God is prescribed only for those whose psyches have not been sufficiently purified and whose intuitive intelligence has not been adequately awakened. Such worship of an object created by themselves as a concept may give the worshippers a certain amount of satisfaction and peace of mind but it is a futile process from the point of view of experiencing one's true nature.

The God who is fit to be worshipped by the highly evolved intellects is one which supports the entire phenomenal creation as its substance ... A God beyond all concepts, infinite and intemporal ... A God which, like the flavor in food, is within every sentient being and therefore needs no seeking ... A God who cannot be comprehended because He transcends the mind and five senses of cognition.

Universal Consciousness is to be worshipped by one's own personal consciousness, not by offering flowers or food or sandalpaste, nor by lighting incense and waving lights. It should be worship without any effort, by Self-realization alone, by the supreme meditation in the continuous, unbroken awareness of the within, the indwelling presence. This worship needs no effort because there is nothing to be attained which one does not already possess.

Worship of the universal Consciousness consists of accepting whole-heartedly whatever comes our way unsought and unsolicited – all physical pleasures and all ailments. It is accepting whatever activities take place through the psychophysical organism. The Self should be worshipped with all of the pleasures that come effortlessly and spon-taneously, whether such pleasures are sanctioned or forbidden by the scriptures, whether considered desirable or undesirable, appropriate or inappropriate. The Self should be worshipped with all experiences, whether beautiful and pleasant or ugly and unpleasant, that arise due to the coincidence of time, circumstance and environment. Experiences should be accepted in a state of equanimity, like the openness of space, with the mind utterly quiescent in infinite expansion within. External actions take place without volition, without desire or rejection. All is witnessed without desire, without rejection, without judging.

THE FINAL TRUTH p. 34

DISPASSION

We find people at different points in the conceptual stream of evolution. Until discrimination and dispassion arise, it is no use trying to get anyone interested in spirituality – he will not be interested. Once the turning point occurs, once dispassion arises, then the personal, identified consciousness – never the illusory individual – turns inward towards its true nature. Then Self-enquiry begins. Thereafter, when conditions are suitable in a particular human apparatus (which could take many, many lives – but not of the same individual 'soul' or whatever name may be given to this illusory entity), the event will occur which is known as enlightenment.

The turning point, the turning or thought back towards the Source, is itself a spontaneous happening over which the supposed individual has no control in any manner or form. It is a part of the dream-play that is called life – the totality of functioning.

Dispassion arises when the heart persistently begins to question the validity of a 'happiness' based on material objects which do not have any kind of consistency or permanence. The same objects which appeared to bring happiness at one time, bring unhappiness at another. The mind then seeks other objects which too suffer from the same deficiency: pleasure and suffering come about from subject/object relationship, which itself is based on certain sentient objects coming together purely by chance. All happiness and misery, based on the desire for certain objects and on relationships with other sentient objects, seems to abide in the mind and the mental attitude. And mind itself is illusory and unreal. It disappears totally in deep sleep or under sedation.

True dispassion is not brought about by austerity or by pilgrimages or by conscious good deeds. It comes only by directly apperceiving one's true nature. The earliest stirrings of dispassion can arise only through what might be called divine Grace. In reality, this means a condition of the psychosomatic mechanism (the supposed individual) that has gradually evolved through many 'lives'. These early stirrings might arise suddenly and spontaneously, but more often they come after an apparent cause, such as some serious difficulty in life or a sudden bereavement in the family.

When dispassion persists and matures, it gradually transforms itself into the spirit of Self-enquiry, which in its turn strengthens dispassion. Indeed, *dispassion, Self-enquiry and Self-realization together form an inseparable combination.*

The question of human effort in relation to the arising of dispassion, leading to divine Grace, which in turn leads to the 'path' of liberation, has always been a puzzling one. The Masters say that without human effort nothing can be achieved. But at the same time they tell us that what is destined to happen will happen. Is there any use in prayer or effort? Should we just remain idle?

What is actually meant by those apparently contradictory statements by the Masters is that it is the feeling 'I do' that is the hindrance. If you are destined to do, you will not be able to avoid it – somehow you will be forced to do. It is really not your choice whether to do or not, because the individual as such does not have the independence or autonomy to have volition.

What constitutes bondage or hindrance to enlightenment is not effort but the sense of doership. This is the point behind the apparent contradiction that the Masters seem to teach predestination in theory but free will in practice. This also explains the affirmation by Christ that not even a sparrow can fall without the will of God, and that the very hairs on one's head are numbered.

The Koran affirms that all power, all knowledge, all Grace, are with God, and that 'He leads aright whom He will and leads astray whom He will.' And yet both Christ and the Koran exhort men to right effort. Perhaps this puzzle would resolve itself when it is seen in the perspective of the totality of functioning proceeding to unfold the play of the Grand Design.

THE FINAL TRUTH pp. 202–4

DOERSHIP

Y ou *do* nothing, and you *don't do nothing*. You merely let whatever happens happen without any sense of having done anything. In other words, 'you' do precisely what you have been doing without the sense of any 'you' doing anything. Everything that happens is merely witnessed, without any comparing or judging by any 'me'.

Someone with a misunderstanding about Jnana would no doubt be horrified to know that 'enjoying life' can exist after the understanding has happened! In fact, what happens is that because of this misunderstanding (which is, of course, part of the what-is), a seeker is afraid to enjoy life, considering it a severe obstacle to enlightenment! What a joke the whole thing is.

It is not easy to forget the persistent query, 'I understand, but having understood, what do I do?!' The answer is: do whatever you feel like doing – live as if you were enlightened. And then suddenly there is the answer that life goes on precisely as it is supposed to, irrespective of what the illusory individual thinks 'he' is doing!!

CONSCIOUSNESS WRITES p. 100

JUST BE. Doing and not doing are both 'doing' – one positive, the other the negative aspect of the 'me's' volition. Trying to do something or not-to-do something brings in the illusory 'me'-concept. It is always the 'me' wanting to do something or not to do.

EXPERIENCING THE TEACHING p. 27

Ashtavakra refers to 'faith' as the only remedy for the snake bite of doership – the faith that the human being exists, not as an individual body-mind entity which is merely a phenomenal object, but as Noumenon, not as an individual object but as the one Subject. Such faith brings about the spontaneous and sudden understanding that 'I' am the one subject and the entire phenomenal manifestation is my objective expression. 'I' am the universal Consciousness within which has spontaneously arisen the totality of the phenomenal manifestation.

In this verse, Ashtavakra goes to the root of the matter. What is it that is at the root of the concept of bondage and unhappiness? It is the sense of doership, the notion of volition. The entire mechanism of what is known as living one's life is based on the notion that whenever a human being acts in any manner – whatever the act – it is because he wants to act in that manner. In other words, it is supposed that volition is behind every act of a human being and that he is therefore 'responsible' for it. The fact of the matter, however, is that human beings usually do not 'act' but 'react' to an outside stimulus. If even a little thought is given to the matter, it will be obvious that very few actions are truly the result of volition or acts of will. Most of the time living, for most people, is conditioned by a series of reflexes based essentially on instinct, habit and even propaganda. The scope of deliberate, considered action is in actual life extremely limited. And yet almost every person firmly believes that he is the doer, and that is why Ashtavakra refers to this notion of individual volition as the bite of the deadly serpent of the ego.

A DUET OF ONE pp. 23–4

What is to be done? Nothing.

Then what happens? 'You', then, are free of the dualism of 'me' and 'not me'. 'You' are at peace *within*, without any sorrow or doubt in mind. 'You' remain firmly established in the inner silence, without any concern for your welfare, content with whatever comes along. 'You' live effortlessly, without either wanting anything or deliberately giving up anything. This is brought about by the firm apprehension that everything happens in Consciousness without any effort by any supposed individual entity, precisely as a mirror reflects the objects around it without any intention. A flight of birds is reflected in the water of the lake but the birds do not *intend* to make a reflection, nor does the water *intend* to reflect the flight of the birds.

When the apperception of Truth occurs, it is realized that whatever comes one's way unsought must be wholeheartedly accepted and enjoyed. Nothing need be abandoned or rejected or given up, because even such renunciation would be volitional. It is realized that while there is nothing to work for, this does not imply deliberate inaction, because deliberate action and inaction are identical. *When the mind ceases to entertain any notion of doership or non-doership, all action becomes non-action.*

THE FINAL TRUTH pp. 53–4

No volitional factor can interfere with the operation of the process of causation. That which is itself the cause of effects – a phenomenal object – cannot introduce a fresh cause (the exercise of volition) in the inexorable chain of causation.

We think in terms of doing something or refraining from doing something with the intention that a subsequent event may or may not occur. This view is based on the misconception that the future depends on our volitional actions today. It is this false premise of autonomy and the retribution or reward, which are the basis of volitional ethics, that make for the chains of our supposed bondage.

EXPERIENCING THE TEACHING pp. 91 & 101

The vocable 'I' – the 'me' who thinks he is the volitional 'do-er' – is what might be called the operational center in the phenomenal sentient object that is known as the human being. Its functional responsibility is to organize and care for the phenomenon it controls. This vocable 'I', or the 'me'-concept, attaches itself to the various emotional impulses that arise (like love, hate, fear, greed, etc.) for the protection and perpetuation of the phenomenon. It represents the psychosomatic mechanism, and this representation gives rise to the identification which is the cause of the supposed bondage. This operational center is called the 'head' in Europe (what Wittgenstein calls 'the little man'), the 'heart' in China (physiologically more relevant), and the *antahkarana* ('mind' including intellect, as the inner equipment) in India.

EXPERIENCING THE TEACHING p. 20

EFFORT

All positive efforts are as futile as trying to see one's face in a mirror that is behind one's back. It is only direct Self-knowledge, resulting from enquiry into the movements arising in one's consciousness, which acts as the *sadguru*, the supreme preceptor. All efforts made by a supposed entity can only lead to frustration. It is only the effortless effort (passive witnessing) along the pathless path (pure understanding without a 'me' as the comprehender) which can lead to the goalless goal ('That' which has always been here and now).

THE FINAL TRUTH p. 204

Self-realization is not available to those who are 'weak'. And, of course, predictably, the word 'weak' has been interpreted as being without the strength and determination to undergo a lot of discipline and hard work. Therefore seekers undergo a lifetime of seeking and still remain confused. What 'weakness' truly means is a lack of courage to give up those traditional routines which were prescribed for when one was a spiritual beginner. It is the lack of courage to accept the intuitive promptings of the basic, fundamental Truth in its totality that all there is, is Consciousness.

A DUET OF ONE p. 97

Effort contained in illusory desire on the part of an illusory individual to achieve an illusory goal! All that was necessary was to turn his gaze inward whereas all his effort was necessarily directed outward. Mind when turned inward ceases to conceptualize, and the ceasing of conceptualizing is tantamount to liberation because the conceptualizing itself was the creation of bondage.

A DUET OF ONE p. 69

This question of individual volition and personal effort is extremely subtle and difficult to understand. And yet it is absolutely necessary not only to understand it intellectually but to absorb it in our very being. Difficulty arises because most Masters seem to have taught pre-destination in theory but free will in practice! Jesus Christ affirmed that without the will of God not even a sparrow can fall, and that the very hairs on one's head are numbered. And the Koran very definitely affirms that all knowledge and power are with God and that He leads aright whom He will and leads astray whom He will. And yet both Christ and the Koran exhort men to right effort and condemn sin. The *apparent* contradiction would easily be solved if one kept in mind the concept of spiritual evolution mentioned above. The absolute illusoriness of the individual human being – and his so-called effort (*pourasha*) – will be quickly understood by the one who is on the very brim of enlightenment, whereas someone who is much lower in the scale will more easily accept the concept of effort, determination and concentration. The one whose *beeja* (seed) is basically action-oriented will tend towards *karma* Yoga because he is what is known as the 'somatotonic' type, whereas the 'cerebrotonic' will at once grasp with delight the principle of non-effort and non-duality without the least danger of misunderstanding. It is undoubtedly because of this inherent and basic difference between the different types of human beings – at different locations in the conceptual evolutionary scale – that the Masters have specifically enjoined that the esoteric teaching of non-duality should not be preached 'in a public place'. There, there would be the distinct possibility of the teaching not only being not understood, but being misunderstood.

So long as a person considers effort as his personal effort, with the purpose of achieving something, he is rejecting the all-mightiness of the Almighty. So long as a person wants something from the Almighty, he is rejecting the fact of the 'Thy will be done'. True love of God means surrender to Him, wanting nothing, not even salvation.

The central point of the ultimate understanding is that at any moment or instant – in any *kshana* – there is perfection in the totality of the functioning. Whatever imperfection is seen, is seen by the imperfect mind in duration and duality. If this is clearly apperceived, no problem can arise, no apparent discrepancy or contradiction can arise.

THE FINAL TRUTH pp. 216–17

Personal effort can only be in duration, which again is the very concept from which liberation is sought into intemporality. Therefore, all that is necessary is the clear realization of what we are, of our true nature which is obnubilated, clouded and darkened by a conditional reflex which identifies the subject *that we are* with the object (the individual) *that we think we are.* Such realization cannot need any effort. It can only be sudden and spontaneous through immediate apperception.

What is meant by 'personal effort' needs some clarification. For instance, Nisargadatta Maharaj would ask someone to practice meditation, while to someone else he might say that meditation could be an obstacle. When he recommended meditation it would generally be to those who complained of an overactive mind always flooded with too many thoughts, much as he might have suggested regular doses of castor oil to someone suffering from chronic constipation. But those who prided themselves on their regular meditation at fixed times for long periods as a means of achieving enlightenment, were warned by Maharaj that their meditation was an impediment and an obstruction for enlightenment to happen. The difference was clear: the intent and purpose behind the meditation. In the latter case, there was an individual 'meditator', meditating with the specific intention of 'achieving' enlightenment for 'himself'. To such meditators, he would say, 'Alright, you meditate and go into samadhi for 10 hours, or 10 days or 10 years or 100 years – but then what? You would still remain in the framework of space-time.' He would give the instance of a Hatha-Yogi who asked his attendant for a meal, and then went into samadhi; he resumed normal Consciousness again after 10 days, and promptly asked the attendant 'Where is my meal?'! Maharaj would therefore warn such meditators that meditation of this kind could be a definite hindrance apart from being useless because it could bring in certain Yogic powers at the meditator's command which could easily bolster up his ego and make him swerve away from his original objective which though misguided was nonetheless laudable. However, when someone explained that he did meditation whenever he felt like it, but without any specific purpose, not meditating on anything in particular but as a means of mental relaxation, and emptying of the mind, Maharaj certainly did not discourage him.

EXPLORATIONS INTO THE ETERNAL p. ix

EGO

The human being has been seeking freedom ('enlightenment', 'Self-realization') from 'bondage' ever since time began for him, and it could be recognized that there never was a time when some of the human beings had not realized this freedom, which is really freedom from the concept of bondage. The reason for this is that this freedom is not achieved; it happens when there is the sudden realization that there just is no individual who is in bondage, that the only bondage is the sense of volition – the belief that the individual is in control of his own life and can do whatever he wants to do. The amazing fact is that the human being holds this belief in spite of the staggering weight of personal experience.

The answer has perhaps been given by Jon Franklin, a Pulitzer Prize writer, when he says: 'The human being is a mechanism in which there is a mechanism which prevents the human mechanism from seeing its mechanistic nature.' This mechanism which prevents the human mechanism from seeing its mechanistic nature has been variously described, but is generally known as the 'ego'. The 'ego', according to my concept, is not merely identification with a name and physical form (as is generally misconceived), but the sense of volition, the sense of personal doership, the sense of individually being in charge.

The problem of an escape from the dungeon of volition has basically been the discursive methods that have been suggested from time to time to acquire the supposedly necessary conceptual knowledge. However, in fact, the understanding is not conceptual knowledge at all, but a sudden, spontaneous, intuitive realization that there really was no 'bondage' other than the mistaken belief that one is individually the thinker, the doer, the experiencer.

The Ultimate Understanding pp. 153–4

The ego-sense (with all its differentiation of me-and-the-other in space-time) arises when Consciousness becomes 'aware of the savor in salt, the sweetness in sugar and the pungency in the chili'. It arises when Consciousness becomes aware of the nature of a rock, a mountain, a tree, a river. It arises when the multifarious combinations of particles and molecules are seen in Consciousness as objects of the pseudo-subject instead of as mere appearances or reflections within itself. In reality there is no subject-object relation because in all such combinations Consciousness is immanent therein.

THE FINAL TRUTH p. 193

Our entire life seems to be nothing but a wasted effort to control our natural responses and reactions to events. The basis of any control is the dualism of the one who controls and that which is controlled. We hardly ever bother to consider who this supposed controller is and what he is supposed to control. The controller is clearly the suppositional entity that intends to change 'what-is' to suit what he thinks are his requirements; and the whole point is that this controller has no identity other than the concept created by thought, by the past and by memory. And what this ego-controller is trying to do is to control something that is also the product of thought. For instance, suppose one is angry about something. The immediate reaction is to suppress the anger or at least to rationalize it; but the fact of the matter is, as Maharaj repeatedly pointed out, that one is not separate from the anger (or any other emotion) because the one who tries to suppress anger and the anger itself are not two separate things but are both appearances or movements in consciousness – *the controller is the controlled*. Living life without control, however, does not mean indulging in whatever you crave for, since the whole point of living naturally without control is living non-volitionally, living without wanting anything consciously or not wanting anything deliberately, living without mentation (reacting mentally), merely witnessing the events as in a dream-play without any involvement. Then, the mind becomes not vacant like that of the idiot but extraordinarily alert, with the brain recording only the facts necessary for practical purposes. Then, the mind becomes free of the usual constant chattering neither because of any conscious control nor due to any chemical action but easily and naturally through the mere understanding of 'what-is'. Then, the mind (which is the content of the personal or individual consciousness) becomes one with the impersonal or universal consciousness, and in spite of all the activity without, remains within in that silence which is not related to either time or space or sound which are all concerned only with the suppositional entity.

EXPLORATIONS INTO THE ETERNAL p. 172

ENLIGHTENMENT

How could enlightenment be anything but sudden? If it were not sudden, then it would be in duration, subject to the conceptual bonds of TIME, and, therefore, necessarily an illusion.

Enlightenment can only be 're-integration in Intemporality'.

THE ULTIMATE UNDERSTANDING p. 25

Enlightenment or awakening is not a state of existence like that of a rock or a vegetable. It is a state which arises consequent on the deepest possible conviction of the unicity of What-Is and of the non-difference between What-Is and what-appears. It arises after a thorough Self-enquiry, at the end of which all mental conditioning of dualism disappears altogether. It is a state of total freedom (*Kaivalya*). All that appears and all that happens is accepted as an integral part of 'What -Is' and there is not the slightest desire to change anything or become anything else.

THE FINAL TRUTH p. 229

Why all the excitement about the state of enlightenment?*

All the excitement exists because the conditioning in man has inverted his viewpoint to an extent that makes him think that the abnormal condition of chaos, unrest and conflict is his normal state. He thinks that the normal state of unfathomable peace and content-ment (glimpses of which he occasionally gets in those rare moments when the mind is free of thoughts) is an abnormal state that must be acquired or attained by special positive efforts.

* These dialogues are not with a questioner. Ramesh sets up the question which he answers in this book.

Does that amount to saying that no one has ever been enlightened?

Yes it does. How could any 'one', any 'you' or any 'me' possibly become enlightened? Of course, a phenomenon – a psychosomatic appearance in consciousness – could certainly *imagine* that he has become enlightened. Precisely as a dreamed phenomenon does in a dream, until he disappears along with all the other phenomena when the dreamer awakes.

But we do talk about sages being enlightened.

We certainly do, but that is part of a lot of nonsense we generally speak and get involved in! Thus it is said that the Buddha attained nirvana. But the Buddha himself said specifically that he had not *attained* anything. Ramana Maharshi repeatedly stated that what people usually call 'realization' or 'enlightenment' already exists. It is not something to be acquired. Therefore, any attempt to attain it would be a self-defeating exercise. But did his visitors believe him?

EXPERIENCING THE TEACHING pp. 37–42

ESCAPES

All escapes, including television and other forms of entertainment, are merely an effort to get away from the identification of the 'me' as the doer and the experiencer. Change of environment may produce a certain kind of temporary relaxation for the body and mind, but greed and envy will continue to rear their heads in any environment and any circumstances. In watching a movie, for instance, the purpose is to forget oneself, but all that happens is that the 'me' gets identified with a character in the movie, and suffers his experiences, pleasures and miseries. Dis-identification is the only answer, and this, says the sage, can only happen when there is a deep understanding that this life and living is only a great dream in which all human beings are thrown in as characters. It is only the Self, the impersonal dreamer witnessing the dream, who transcends the doing and the experiencing in the dream. The dreamed character can do nothing about the events in the dream. You identify yourself with the dreamed character as the doer and the experience, and you suffer the consequences of the doing, which is the experiencing. You dis-identify yourself from the dreamed character and you instantly become the Self, the Subject. You are the dreamer merely witnessing the objective manifestation, so long as the dreamed manifestation exists.

A DUET OF ONE p. 179

EVOLUTION

Where the intellect is immature, and the individual keeps seeking (and wanting) enlightenment as an object for himself or herself, the wanting and the seeking continues to be the bondage.

The various reactions to the same statement of Truth are themselves the spiritual evolution constantly happening in the impersonal functioning of Totality. Individual human beings are merely the instruments through which this evolution is taking place. This evolution begins with Consciousness identifying itself with each individual being as a separate entity. The identification continues through several lives, seeking pleasure through sense objects. Then suddenly in a particular body-mind organism appears the sense of dispassion for sense-objects, and the process of dis-identification, the seeking, begins and continues through several lives. Finally the process ends in a total dis-identification with a body-mind organism as a separate entity. Enlightenment happens as an impersonal event in Consciousness through the instrument of a particular body-mind organism which has been conceived and created as one evolved highly enough to be able to receive the sudden apperception. It is necessary to understand two important aspects of this spiritual evolution:
   a) the evolution is an impersonal process in the functioning of Totality, and, therefore,
   b) no individual entity can be concerned as a separate doer in order to achieve enlightenment.

Sudden enlightenment does produce a certain change in outlook and perspective for the 'individual' body-mind organism, particularly in the interim period between what a Taoist sage terms as 'enlightenment' and 'deliverance'. Even after enlightenment happens, the individual must necessarily continue to function as a separate body-mind organism during the remainder of its span of life. There can, of course, be no hard and fast rule concerning the changes that will be brought about by the fact of enlightenment having happened. By and large, the individual concerned will continue to live as he did before, but it is not at all unlikely that his zest for pleasure will undergo a subtle change. He may be found to be not such 'good company' as he was before. He may be found to enjoy his solitude more. Such changes are bound to take place because while the identity with the individual body must necessarily continue for the body to function in life, what is absent is the sense of doership, the sense of a separate entity. In other words, while the individual continues to live his life more or less as before, there is no longer any personal involvement in anything that happens. Whatever happens may have an immediate reaction, but it is very much on the surface, like a gentle wave on the surface of a lake. Whatever happens is merely witnessed, without any feeling of personal involvement.

A DUET OF ONE pp. 100–1

In the course of spiritual evolution (which may involve many 'lives' but not the same individual *jiva*) the process culminating in the phenomenon of enlightenment could be *notionally* broken up or analyzed into seven stages. First, there is the thought that material pleasure is much too transitory and unstable, and that a more stable and lasting kind of happiness should be sought. This gives rise to the process of Self-enquiry which may include a search for and guidance from one or more gurus. At this stage, there arises a keen sense of dispassion and non-attachment, because of which the mind becomes more sensitive, more subtle and more transparent. After these three stages, there *arises* a deeper dispassion, a *natural* turning away from sense-objects, and a firmer attachment towards one's real nature, whatever it might be. This attachment towards Truth takes a firmer hold of the psyche and makes it rooted, in the fifth stage, in one's true Self. The sixth stage arises when the mind, deeply rooted in the Self, ceases conceptualizing and objectivizing. The world of appearance is seen as merely the reflection of one's own true Self. The ultimate seventh stage means continuously living in the present moment (noumenal state), without any sense of doership, like dry leaf in the breeze. This is the transcendental stage, where everything is spontaneous, natural, unbroken.

THE FINAL TRUTH p. 205

No rational or logical explanation is possible in regard to the totality of functioning and the ways of providence. The divided mind, which functions in the duality of life, is incapable of understanding the whole Mind (Consciousness) which is its own source. The shadow cannot know its own substance. An Einstein does not occur suddenly. The brain capable of receiving the theory of relativity 'from outside' (as Einstein has himself said) could not possibly have been developed in one lifetime. The conditions necessary in a human apparatus to be able to produce the *Jnaneshwari* and the *Amritanubhava* at the age of sixteen could not have been produced in a Jnaneshwar in one lifetime. The conditions necessary for sudden enlightenment are produced after several lifetimes. But the series of lifetimes necessary for the final event of Self-realization does not occur to any single 'soul' or entity for the simple reason that all there is at any moment is nothing but Consciousness. No sentient being can have any volition or independence of choice and action because there is no such thing.

The course of evolution is seen all the time in life. There are some people who are so absorbed in chasing what they consider as 'happiness' that they do not have either the time or inclination to stop and wonder if their kind of happiness is truly worth having.

THE FINAL TRUTH p. 201

FAITH

Trust in God – acceptance of Consciousness as the ultimate reality in the functioning of the universe – makes life simple for the man of understanding. In the absence of a personal sense of doership the man of understanding does not engage in a self-conscious and deliberate campaign to 'do his duty' with the intention of acquiring happiness. Indeed he has come to the conviction that the whole concept of happiness and unhappiness is based on the world of objects and is thus in effect quite illusory and transitory.

The understanding that Consciousness (or God) is in charge of the functioning of the universe brings with it the simple good and the virtuous with which one is endowed by the very fact of being conscious – I AM. 'I am' is reality. 'I am so-and-so' is false, which brings with it the delusion of a sense of personal doership.

With this 'Trust in God', grows quietly the humility and simplicity of the ordinary life of faith, which is a matter of seeing the good as it exists – the What Is – rather than as something to be achieved through one's own effort. This happens as the result of the understanding that, as the Buddha has put it, there are events and deeds but no individual doer thereof. If there is no individual doer – and all actions are part of the functioning of Totality (or God's actions) – then my actions are not my own. More important, the actions of someone else are not his or her actions either – and therefore how can I consider anyone my enemy? With this basic understanding arises, naturally and spontaneously, humility, love and compassion. These are not virtues to be deliberately acquired – they cannot be acquired by personal effort. They are a gift from God which come as a result of the simple, basic understanding.

THE BHAGAVAD GITA pp. 9–10

Trust in God – acceptance of consciousness as the ultimate reality in the functioning of the universe – makes life simple for the man of understanding. In the absence of a personal sense of doership, the man of understanding does not engage in a self-conscious and deliberate campaign to 'do his duty' with the intention of acquiring happiness. Indeed, he has come to the conviction that the whole concept of happiness and unhappiness is based on the world of objects and is thus in effect quite illusory and transitory. This would be true also of the more refined concepts like 'justice and injustice', 'virtue and vice', 'good and evil' or 'right and wrong'. He is fully aware that the moment these concepts are treated as objects to be achieved, they lead to delusion.

RIPPLES p. 37

Ashtavakra refers to 'faith' as the only remedy for the snake bite of doership – the faith that the human being exists, not as an individual body-mind entity which is merely a phenomenal object, but as Noumenon, not as an individual object but as the one Subject. Such faith brings about the spontaneous and sudden understanding that 'I' am the one subject and the entire phenomenal manifestation is my objective expression. 'I' am the universal Consciousness within which has spontaneously arisen the totality of the phenomenal manifestation.

A DUET OF ONE p. 24

Faith is the power which is capable of bringing about the spontaneous apperception of the truth. Faith intuitively recognizes the ring of truth, and opens 'the eye of the heart' to apperceive the Truth.

Faith is based on a certain inescapable inevitability, a relaxed acceptance of What-Is, totally free of any doubt or opinion.

A DUET OF ONE pp. 18–19

FEAR

The basis of all fear is the entity, the identification with a particular body as a *separate* individual with autonomy and independence, with volition and choice. Fear, desire and all other forms of affectivity are mere manifestations of the pseudo-entity which constitutes pseudo-bondage, and what needs to be eliminated is this pseudo-entity rather than the manifestations of that pseudo-entity.

Fear arises from the 'other' because the 'other' is always in opposition to the 'Self'. It is therefore 'dualism' which is the basis of all fear. There cannot be the 'other' concept unless there is first the 'me' concept. How does duality arise? It is the mechanism for the phenomenal manifestation of the universe. What we are noumenally is consciousness-at-rest, the whole or the undivided mind. When consciousness stirs into movement, the whole mind gets divided into two elements – a subject which perceives and cognizes, and an object which is perceived and cognized. This duality is the very basis of the objectivization of the subjective noumenon. In this objectivization, all are objects and therefore when one object perceives and cognizes another, the former *assumes* subjectivity and considers his subjective function to be a separate entity as a 'self' and the perceived object as the 'other', although in reality both cognizer and the cognized exist only in the mind in which the process of objectivization occurs and, as such, can have existence only in relation to each other (as interdependent opposites) and never any independent and autonomous existence.

A study of the anatomy of fear would enable us to understand more clearly the phenomenon of fear itself. Both the interrelated manifestations of aggressiveness and fear have their base in desire; the need for the gratification of desire causes aggressiveness and fear arises because of the possibility of not achieving such gratification. Remove desire, and there is neither the aggressiveness for achievement nor the fear of failure. The physical aspects of the phenomenon of fear are simple enough. It is an allied aspect of the instinct of self-preservation and is as useful as the reflex that keeps one from being scorched or prepares one to face the imminent danger of being attacked by someone. But this is totally different from the psychological fear or anxiety about not achieving something acceptable or something unacceptable being forced upon us. Such kind of fear soon becomes a habit which keeps infusing toxicity into the biological system and, over a period, ruins the very mechanism of the psychosomatic apparatus that constitutes our body; and this, of course, adversely affects the performance of that apparatus, which in turn further increases the fear and its effect on the body. Realization that such psychological fear is merely an aspect of affectivity (to which only the conceptual ego is susceptible) breaks this vicious circle. Such a realization brings about the dis-identification from the ego and creates a feeling of emptiness or hollowness and a sense of freedom from anxiety, which in turn releases an extraordinary amount of energy (that would otherwise have been wasted) which cannot but improve our day-to-day performance beyond recognition: it is so much easier to float with the tide than swim against the current.

EXPLORATIONS INTO THE ETERNAL pp. 70–4

FREE WILL

Nobody likes being told that he has no free will. And yet look at the state of the world at the present time. The world is on the brink of disaster, where it has been for many years now with one crisis after another. The question – the big question – therefore remains: The human being certainly has tremendous intelligence (to send a man to the moon); he is also supposed to have free will – then why has the human being been unable to combine his intelligence and his free will to make the world a better place?!

There is also another aspect. There are so many intelligent people, leaders in their respective fields, who are very much interested in knowing their future. If they really believed in their own free will, why would they be so interested in astrology and similar phenomena?!

If you think along these lines, the only reasonable conclusion you will arrive at is that the human being has been acting in this fashion because he has no control over his thoughts and emotions. What he considers as *his* actions are in fact only *reactions* of the individual organism to an outside impulse: a thought which occurs, an event that he sees or perhaps what he happens to hear. Each organism reacts according to the natural characteristics with which it has been programmed: physical, mental, intellectual, temperamental.

Another difficulty about truly accepting this teaching is the argument that it leads to a 'fatalistic' attitude. The fatalistic argument translates itself into the question: 'If I am not to be motivated by the fruits of my action, and, indeed, if I have no free will over my actions, why should I work at all?' The answer is astonishingly simple: you will not be able to be inactive for any length of time because the energy within the organism will compel you to act: to act according to the natural characteristics of the organism. In other words, whether to act or not is itself not in your control.

The essence of the ultimate understanding is the ineluctable fact that the individual human being, *as such*, does not – cannot – have any volition. He is without any independence of choice of decision and action, for the simple reason that the human being is not an autonomous entity. The human being is merely an infinitesimal part of the totality of manifestation. That the human being can see, hear, etc. through his senses is merely because he has, like any other sentient being (insect or animal), been endowed with sentience. That he can think is merely because he has, in addition, been endowed with intellect. In the absence of consciousness, there is no sentience, no intellect, and as far as the human being is concerned, no manifest world.

THE FINAL TRUTH p. 215

Knowing that he cannot live according to his will or volition, that he is in fact 'being lived' (as an instrument of the Totality), he also knows the futility of 'intentions'. By abstaining from volition the man of wisdom is free of anxiety and misery, because then he transcends con-ceptualization which is the basis of volition and intention. Knowing that he is being lived, the man of wisdom transcends both volitional action and its counterpart, volitional non-action: volitional non-doing is also doing. It is for this reason that the man of wisdom goes about his business in the ordinary way without any intentions, without any sense of doership.

It is only the 'me'-concept that can have intentions because 'will' and 'ego' are synonymous terms. Thus the absence of volition in the case of the man of wisdom does not mean phenomenal inaction but the absence of volitional action (positive or negative). The absence of volitional phenomenal action can only mean the presence of noumenal action. In other words, the non-volitional action of the man of wisdom (whether perceptive, conceptive, or somatic) is noumenal action, the non-action of the sage (because the 'me' and his intention is totally absent).

A DUET OF ONE p. 83

GOD

'I Am that I Am', said Jahweh. And, He said it on behalf of all of us: other than 'this which I Am,' nothing ever was, nothing is, and nothing could ever be.

THE ULTIMATE UNDERSTANDING p. 143

The greatest freedom to find is freedom from the fear of God: I do nothing; He does everything.

THE ULTIMATE UNDERSTANDING p. 75

If you stop fearing God, it is more than likely that you will start loving God.

THE ULTIMATE UNDERSTANDING p. 20

You never need fear God. No human object ever had the power to do anything against God's will.

THE ULTIMATE UNDERSTANDING p. 40

Says Ramakrishna Paramahaunsa: 'He who comes to know that he is only an instrument in the hands of the Lord, has no egoistic feeling. He is aware that he is only a tool with which God has His work done.* Such a man causes harm to nobody. The poison of egoism is no more in him. A steel knife becomes a gold knife with the touch of the philosopher's stone. Though the form of the knife is there, it is not useful any more for cutting. Similarly, the *jnani* retains a seeming individuality, but no ignorance-born activity occurs in and through him.'

* *Bhagavad Gita*, ch. v, v. 15.

The Omnipresent Lord does not take note of the merit or demerit of anyone. What-is is always perfect. The light of the *Atman* is covered by the darkness of delusion, and that is how the human beings are deluded.

This verse firmly demolishes the concept of a God sitting somewhere in the clouds, peeping down and keeping a perfect account of every sin and every good deed done by every single human being, so that an individual may be punished or rewarded in due course. It should be clear that such a concept is steeped in ignorance. Such a concept cannot prevail if one is totally convinced that no action can happen except by God's will. If God's will is totally accepted, one's personal will cannot exist, and therefore, there cannot be any question of any sin or merit.

Such a concept is bound to evoke immediately an argument such as this: 'If it is God's will that I should commit a murder, why should I be punished for it?'! The answer is astonishingly simple: there is no 'you' to be punished or rewarded; it was God's will, and the destiny of that human organism, that the murder would be committed, and it is also God's will, and the destiny of *that organism*, to be punished for the act.

The only will that can prevail at any time is God's will, and to see that he himself (the individual) is merely an instrument operated upon by God. It is a matter of either a total surrender to God, or a strong sense of personal choice, personal doership and personal responsibility: one is knowledge, the other is ignorance.

THE BHAGAVAD GITA pp. 58–62

It must be realized that whatever anyone seeks must be seen as the seeking happening through an individual human organism as its God-given destiny. Then it will be seen that there is truly no individual seeker who could be proud of being a spiritual seeker. If someone seeks money and power, it is because God wants him to do so. If a man seeks spirituality, again, it is because there is God's Grace.

Not every seeker can aspire for total perfection. It is a matter of Divine Will: all he can do is to accept this Divine Will and not let his desire for freedom itself become an obstruction. What this means is that the seeker must surrender to God's will in regard to the entire process of awakening. That he is a seeker is itself because of God's Grace: surrender to this Grace, and leave everything to that will.

A similar encouragement is voiced by Ramana Maharshi when he tells the seeker: 'Your head is already in the tiger's mouth, there is no escape.' Why be impatient?!

THE BHAGAVAD GITA pp. 67–8

When most people speak of God or divinity they generally mean the inevitable, the unknown beyond their supposed control and beyond the events of natural order. They pray for the acceptable to happen and the unacceptable not to happen. Others refer to God or divine grace as that which brings about equanimity and the cessation of the fleeting joy and sorrow.

THE FINAL TRUTH p. 54

Blasphemy is any and every action done otherwise than in the presence of God. This is clearly stated in the *Bhagavad Gita*. And let it be clear, by the presence of God, I do *not* mean the presence of an object, an idol. Irrespective of the presence or absence of an object, an idol, *what the 'presence of God' means is the absence of the presence of the self*. It means the immanent divinity.

EXPERIENCING THE TEACHING p. 117

There is no power on earth that is greater than consciousness, the source of sentience and of all thought, and, therefore, it is to consciousness that man must direct his appeal and prayers for all that he needs. In other words, where God abides let us hasten: Consciousness is where God abides – indeed consciousness IS GOD.

Therefore, much as thought might try to brush it aside, the persistent, nagging question remains: if God created the universe, who created God? The very question is pregnant with a sense of blasphemy and guilt for the adult but the innocent infant at a certain age is not satisfied with any superficial answer with which the adult might try to fob him off. What has in fact happened is that man has conceptualized God in the *image of himself* attributing to it the noblest sentiments and qualities that he himself wants but lacks. To reach *that-which-Is* beyond God, intellect is powerless.

Most of the near-perfect actions or performances, and almost all the works of creativity happen in this state of egolessness, when the tenet 'Thy Will be Done' is actually put into practice. It is in the absence of the ego, in the absence of intellectual and psychic effects, that the whole mind takes over the individual action as part of the total functioning and reaches near perfection.

EXPLORATIONS INTO THE ETERNAL p. 156

I am the *Atman* that dwells in the heart of every mortal creature: I am the beginning, I am the life-span, and I am the end of all beings.

BHAGAVAD GITA ch. 10, v. 20

This is the central theme of the *Bhagavad Gita*, and Lord Krishna states this in forceful terms.

The meaning is very clear and this is one of the verses on which meditation could be based with much success.

THE BHAGAVAD GITA p. 90

GOOD

To put the idea in the words of the Lao-Tzu, 'when everyone recognizes goodness as good, there is already evil.' To see this is to understand that seeking good to the exclusion of evil, seeking beauty to the exclusion of ugliness is like seeing the stars to the exclusion of space, seeing the print in a book to the exclusion of the white background, seeking to hold water in a sieve, seeking to avoid the left by persistently turning to the right and thus going around in circles. In spite of the simplest logic in this principle of polarity – or perhaps because of it! – we are inclined to ignore it altogether out of hand because our conditioning clearly indicates to us that unless we constantly keep on trying to improve everything, including ourselves, the only possible end would be sliding back to a lazy chaos: if sufficient and successful effort is not made by 'me', the 'others' would overtake me. It is astonishing that we ignore our actual experience which proves the contrary inasmuch as, for instance, more and more success, more and more money, better and better cars and gadgets, more and more luxury in qualitative and quantitative terms have not brought us a sense of either total achievement or total satisfaction; in fact one finds oneself holding a tiger by the tail. Is there really a choice?

Our conventional thinking and our way of life based thereon make us take the view that it is one or the other – either the pursuit of the good and the beautiful or wallowing in the evil and the ugly. The fact, however, is that there really is no choice because both are insepa-rable elements in living. The human situation is not unlike what has been described as that of the 'fleas on a hot griddle': the flea who falls must jump and the flee who jumps must fall! It is not a case of fatalism based on frustration; the inevitability of the duality of inter-related opposites is what exists.

EXPLORATIONS INTO THE ETERNAL p. 210

What is generally forgotten while considering the subject of 'evil' is the fact that no amount of research can eradicate 'evil' because that is the interconnected opposite of 'good' – both are concepts that form the very basis of the functioning of manifestation, or life as we know it. While the ego of most of the population of the world functions in the creation of 'evil', the ego of a comparatively few people has realized that it is its sense of personal doership or volition which is the cause of the 'evil' in the world; and it is these few people who produce the 'good' as the balancing counterpart in phenomenal life of its opposite, the 'evil'.

To what extent the balancing between 'good' and 'evil' operates at any moment would obviously depend on the Will of the Source or Creator or God, which can be taken to function according to a conceptual Cosmic Law that no created object in the phenomenal universe could possibly fathom.

At all times, in all places, there have been 'good' people doing what they thought they should do. At all times in all places, there have been 'evil' people doing what they thought they should do.

Nothing could have happened unless it was supposed to happen, according to God's Will, according to a conceptual Cosmic Law. Is there really any need for anyone to concern oneself with what is happening according to God's Will, according to Cosmic Law?

Would it not be simpler to witness the divine show – *lila* in all its magnificence and diversity – while continuing to do what one thinks one should do?

THE ULTIMATE UNDERSTANDING pp. 161–2

GRACE

To be a seeker is itself a matter of God's Grace, and the further progress in the process is also a matter of God's Grace.

When the dark ignorance is destroyed by the lamp of knowledge through the *Buddhi-Yoga*, the Yoga of knowledge and discrimination, the Self stands revealed in its own glory as the One-without-a-second, all pervading in its fullness. This ultimate happening is entirely a matter of God's Grace and not something achievable by the devotee through his own efforts.

THE BHAGAVAD GITA p. 89

In regard to Grace, Aldous Huxley has something very pertinent to say: 'The help received by those who devotedly adore or pray to some personal saint, deity or Avatar is often not a genuinely spiritual grace, but a human grace [I might add that even this 'human grace' is part of the spontaneous process of spiritual evolution], coming back to the worshipper from the vortex of psychic power set up by repeated acts of faith, yearning and imagination.'

Spiritual Grace cannot be received continuously or in its fullness, except by those who have willed away their self-will.'

Unless, therefore, the covering of *rajas* and *tamas*, that prevents the pure shining of *sattva*, is removed by the Grace of direct perception, true apperception cannot take place.

A DUET OF ONE pp. 200 & 204

THE GURU

Having earlier gone into the true nature of Shiva-Shakti, the parents of this manifested universe, and into the mechanism of manifestation itself, Jnaneshwar proceeds to explain the true nature of the *Sadguru* without whose explicit blessings one's efforts towards liberation from the worldly bondage would not be successful. It is a tradition in India that the *Sadguru* having apperceived and experienced the Unicity that is the supreme subjectivity and having merged with that Unicity, is one with it and must, therefore, in a relative sense, be worshipped as Unicity.

This point needs a thorough and deep investigation. On the surface it does seem unacceptable that one's efforts to understand and realize the Truth cannot be successful without the help and the 'grace' of someone else. This is because, as Nisargadatta Maharaj used to tell his visitors repeatedly, the seeker regards himself as a separate individual with independent and autonomous existence, and the Guru as another individual with similar separate existence. Maharaj used to say that so long as this attitude prevailed, whatever else one did to attain 'liberation' would not only be utterly useless but would result in a tightening of the 'bondage'. Why so? Because we have always been what-we-are, that is the 'substance', and never, even for a fleeting moment, what-we-think-we are, which is mere 'shadow' without any independent existence.

EXPERIENCE OF IMMORTALITY p. 43

The very necessity of a Guru and the existence of the Guru-disciple relationship arises only from the viewpoint of the disciple who cannot help seeing things from the standpoint of duality. And the problem for him will remain unsolved so long as his seeking continues on the basis of an individual seeking something through the help and 'grace' of another individual called a Guru. The problem can only be dissolved when there is the realization that the apparent individual human being, seeking another apparent individual human being as a Guru, in order to achieve an apparent state of being, is only a part of the impersonal functioning of the totality of manifestation. It is not seeing the matter in this perspective that causes all the terrible misery for the individual seeker who thinks that the seeking is his personal choice and that the success of the quest will depend upon his own efforts to achieve the grace of the Guru.

The relationship between you and me as the disciple and the Guru will take various shapes and concepts in the mind as it intensifies gradually, stays intensified for a while, and then almost fades away from the mind.

The *Sadguru* within – the WITHIN *is* the *Sadguru*, the ONE who brings the teacher and the disciple together as one event – has done it.

The 'you' and the 'Guru' both go so much in the background that there is no difference between the Guru and the disciple, for the simple reason that there IS no difference between them: both are objective expressions of the same singular subjectivity. And yet, so long as the body-mind exists, a 'feeling' of intense intimate relationship continues to exist in a ghostlike manner between the Guru and the disciple.

CONSCIOUSNESS WRITES p. 15

The strain of the effort of the seeker who has engaged in various forms of *sadhana* disappears into the peace of contentment on meeting the Guru – just as the turbulence of the Ganga disappears when the river meets the ocean.

It is only until he meets his Guru that the seeker continues to see the world as something different from himself. As soon as the seeker meets his Guru and gets his blessing, the otherness merges into his own oneness.

Out of compassion for the seeker, the Guru has given up his oneness and assumed the relationship of Guru-disciple and in doing so absorbs the dualism of the disciple unto himself.

Having turned the disciple into his own likeness, the Guru no longer considers himself the Guru as distinct from the disciple, but from the point of view of the disciple, the relationship continues to exist till the end of life.

The grace of the Guru happens when the disciple surrenders everything he has, including his individuality, at the Guru's feet, and in this grace of the Guru merges the triad of giver, giving, and that which is given – the seeker, the seeking, and that which is sought. There is, in short, the final fulfillment of the efforts which had until then remained unfulfilled.

In the absence of the Guru's grace, all the knowledge in the Vedas will be fruitless. The sun of the Guru's grace dispels all the darkness of the intellectual seeking and brings about the fulfillment of all seeking.

It is in the basic illusion of the phenomenal manifestation that the Guru acquires the role of the Guru in relation to the disciple; he brings home to the disciple the nature of the basic illusion and thus rescues the disciple from drowning in the illusory ocean of ignorance.

The Guru demolishes the individuality of the disciple and instead showers on him his own love and compassion in a manner that dissolves the distinction between the Guru and the disciple. Then there remains only the basic Unicity.

And when this happens, to whom can the disciple pay his respects in the absence of any duality between the two? Does the sun have to rise or set? Is he not always the shining star? The Guru remains as the basic Unicity even while performing his role as the Guru in relation to his disciple.

The relationship of the Guru and disciple is like the getting together of the wick and the light – there is only the light. When the camphor and the fire are brought together, both eventually disappear. So when the disciple meditates upon the nature of the Guru, both get merged in each other and all duality disappears.

The Guru's love is so mysterious that even though he is beyond the parameters of all interrelated opposites, he uses the persona of duality to express his love. The Guru brings about an apparent duality in the relationship with the disciple without in any way losing his basic Unicity.

The Guru's Unicity is the repository of all dualities including truth and illusion, knowledge and ignorance: the ocean supports the addition of water through rivers and also its depletion through evaporation; the sun, being Light itself, knows not either darkness or non-darkness. Therefore, the word 'Guru' includes both Guru and disciple.

Only he who is able to see his face without the need of the mirror will understand this mysterious working of the Guru. The Guru expresses his love and compassion in the apparent duality of the Guru-disciple relationship without ever losing his basic Unicity.

RIPPLES pp. 10–13

To begin with, the guru here acknowledges the fact that all he can do is to point to the Truth. He cannot hand over enlightenment as a gift on a platter to the disciple. So long as the identification with a body-mind organism as a separate individual entity continues, the identified pseudo-subject must remain in bondage. Apart from stating the Truth as clearly as possible, after 'showing your true nature as if in a mirror', as Nisargadatta Maharaj used to say, there is nothing more that the guru can do. He can only wait for the disciple to receive and absorb the Truth. The problem is made immensely more difficult by the fact that there is precious little that the disciple himself can 'do' in a positive way.

A DUET OF ONE p. 29

The very first question of the disciple is intensely significant to the guru. It tells him the general level and conditioning of the disciple. It tells him at what point in the spiritual evolution the disciple is at that moment. What is it that the disciple is truly seeking? That is what interests the guru most because on that will depend the guru's answers and advice. Nisargadatta Maharaj asked me, when I first met him, what I wanted from him. My answer was, 'I am not interested in happiness and unhappiness in this world or any other world. What I want to know from you is that Truth, that unchangeable Truth which has always existed and will always exist, irrespective of any prophet or any religion.' Maharaj looked at me intently for a while, then smiled and changed the subject. By that time, others had come into the room and the usual session was about to start.

A certain amount of confusion and misunderstanding comes about because an important point is not always borne in mind regarding the relevance of the guru's answer. The guru is not really concerned with answering the disciple's question as such. The guru is truly concerned with the conditioning under which the disciple suffers, and the disciple's questions reveal this conditioning. The guru is primarily concerned with removing this conditioning. The disciple is initially concerned with 'acquiring' knowledge as such at an intellectual level. The guru is fully aware that there is no such thing as ignorance which could be removed by the acquisition of knowledge. He knows that every individual is the universal Consciousness which has identified itself with the individual body-mind organism, and that such identification is itself the ignorance that the disciple talks about. The disciple *thinks* that it is the acquisition of knowledge which will get rid of the ignorance while the guru *knows* that ignorance is itself the result of the positive action of identification. Any further positive action on the part of the illusory individual, such as any practices or disciplines, would only make the identification stronger.

A DUET OF ONE p. 13

It is indeed a fact that 'devotees all over the world can testify to the limitless stream of guidance one receives when the guru becomes a part of their lives'. It is also a fact that the prevailing coincidences and synchronicities exercise a certain fascination over the 'one' concerned, along with a concurrent concern or uneasiness over this very fascination. As in your case, almost again concurrently, will arise the antidote to this uneasiness with the realization that there is indeed a clear disassociation with the fascination. When the understanding is deep, again as in your case (certainly after a *lot* of pain and frustration), the core of the fascination is not the sense of achievement, but a feeling of gratitude and surrender to the guru or Consciousness or Totality or God.

CONSCIOUSNESS TO CONSCIOUSNESS p. 21

The individuality of the seeker gradually disappears, but in the process, the Guru's grace, which is always present like the shining sun, becomes one with consciousness. The sooner the identification with the body as a separate entity is lost the sooner will the Guru's grace bloom in the consciousness of the disciple. And then he will realize that the Guru is none other than the consciousness within, and it is consciousness which, pleased with the faith and love of the disciple, will act as the *Sadguru* and unfold all the knowledge that is necessary. However, there cannot be any progress (though 'progress' itself is an erroneous concept) if you continue to regard yourself as an entity and expect the Guru, as another entity, to give you some homework to do, and when that is duly completed, to award you a sort of certificate, or something, on a platter as 'liberation'. This whole concept is misconceived. You must realize the true significance of the Guru and his grace before the ever-present Guru's grace can smoothly and naturally flow towards you.

EXPLORATIONS INTO THE ETERNAL p. 61

The *Sadguru*, it is possible, would say it is even sometimes necessary to have more than one Guru according to one's circumstances, according to one's spiritual development and according to one's inherent tendencies. But the essential point to remember is that from the point of view of the Guru, there are no disciples as such because he does not regard any one as being outside of himself; it is only from the point of view of the seeker that there is a Guru. The grace of the Guru is like an ocean – it is entirely up to the disciple how much of the ocean he wants and how much he can carry! And even this is only a concept. Truly there is no duality of Guru and disciple, and this realization brings the search to an end.

The problem, however, would seem to persist from the point of view of the seeker inasmuch as several questions remain unanswered. For example, how is a seeker to recognize his Guru from the numerous spiritual teachers he may come across? Or, assuming that a seeker decides on a particular person as a competent Guru by the peace of mind he felt in his presence and the respect he felt for him, what would be the position if that person turned out not to be suitable as far as that particular seeker is concerned? Presumably, the fate of the seeker in such a situation would be decided according to the degree of his own preparedness and merit. There is also the point that whilst the seeker himself saw no improvement in himself despite his following the Guru's instructions, it may well be that there had actually been considerable improvement though it was not apparent to the seeker. And then, of course, who is to decide upon the suitability and competency or otherwise of the Guru? Finally, there remains the question: 'Who is to be accepted as a Guru?' In the traditional sense of the word, a Guru is one who has been 'invested' with the authority to initiate disciples and prescribe a routine discipline for them; and in this sense a valid investiture would seem to be necessary to lend authority to him as a Guru, whether or not he is truly self-realized. There is, ultimately, the most interesting statement of Bhagavan Ramana Maharshi when a reference was made to the fact that he himself had no Guru as such. Ramana Maharshi said: 'It depends on what you mean by the term GURU; he need not necessarily have a human form, and I might have even had such a Guru at some time or other; and also, did I not sing hymns to the Arunachala hill?'

EXPLORATIONS INTO THE ETERNAL p. 4

HAPPINESS

There is full awareness that the human being is 'being lived' as an intrinsic part of the totality of functioning in the universe. This is what Ashtavakra means when he says 'be happy' or 'live happily' because then there is no volition, there is no sense of doership, no sense of guilt or bondage. In other words, living happily means living naturally, living spontaneously, responding to external situations without any planning, without any preconceived notions – in short, without the interference of the mind. Such a response will naturally bring about physical activity but there will be no sense of doership, no illusion of volition, because the physical activity does not involve any mental activation. In short, the response will be spontaneous without volitional interference, and will therefore lead to awakening to enlightenment. In the absence of volitional involvement, whatever happens is an integral part of the noumenal functioning, the essence of which is mere witnessing of an event without any judging. Judging presupposes duality, whereas witnessing is beyond duality.

Ashtavakra continues:

> **The one who considers himself free is indeed free**
> **while the one who considers himself bound remains**
> **in bondage. The saying 'As one thinks so one**
> **becomes' is certainly a true one.**

A DUET OF ONE p. 26

Ashtavakra gives an amazingly simple formula for being happy in this world. Happiness is important because if you are unhappy in this world, it will be impossible to reach the stage of 'liberation'. In fact, the various qualities or virtues which he has enumerated have an ascending scale leading ultimately to Truth. What Ashtavakra is actually telling his intelligent disciple is that the root of all trouble, that which prevents the seeing of Truth is 'desire'. Later in the dialogue, he makes it clear that desire in any form is the only obstacle, even if the desire is for liberation! The basis of the desire for liberation is the ignorance about the Truth that there never has been any bondage from which liberation could be desired. Bondage is a concept and therefore liberation is also a concept.

A DUET OF ONE p. 15

HUMILITY

Genuine humility is that which is not recognized as such by the one who has it.

THE ULTIMATE UNDERSTANDING p. 65

Do not try too hard to show your humility. The very effort exposes your pride. True humility lies in the absence of doership.

THE ULTIMATE UNDERSTANDING p. 15

What is the basis on which spontaneity works so effectively? The answer in one word would be HUMILITY, but not in the sense in which it is generally used. What is usually called 'humility' happens to be in fact nothing but inverted pride or negative pride, whereas the only implication of true humility is the utter absence of any entity either to be proud or not to be proud.

EXPLORATIONS INTO THE ETERNAL p. 224

HYPNOSIS

A human being, tortured by lust, ambition, competitive conflicts, cannot achieve the peace and tranquillity that is sought, whatever 'spiritual' path he is advised to follow. The only way peace and tranquillity can happen is when the mind is stilled at its very source, when there is the realization that the entire manifestation and its functioning – life as we know it – is an illusion based on an earlier illusion of space and time. If space-time itself is non-existent, being only a concept, how can the manifestation, and a part of it – an object called a human being with its sense of personal doership – be anything but an illusion, *maya*, a divine hypnosis? It is only this deep apperception which can result in a really still mind, a silent mind, which itself is the peace that is sought after so avidly.

THE ULTIMATE UNDERSTANDING p. 76

The fact that we, as separate individual entities, expect to transform ourselves into perfect 'enlightened' personages shows the extent to which we have been conditioned by *Maya*, the power of the Divine hypnosis which has created the 'me's'. 'We' are only phenomena, dreamed characters playing out their respective roles. How can an appearance perfect itself? How can a psychosomatic apparatus, a conditioned body-mind organism perfect itself? Only awakening can make the dreamed character disappear; only dis-identification with the sense of personal doership in a supposed entity can bring about re-cognition of our true identity. And this cannot happen until our conceptual volition has been truly and totally surrendered.

THE ULTIMATE UNDERSTANDING pp. 38–9

What distinguishes a human being from an animal is his capacity to conceptualize, to objectivize, his capacity to form concepts. And he abuses this capacity outrageously. The human being thinks that the universe begins and ends with himself. The human being exults that the smallpox germ has been eliminated, but in this exultation he does not see the situation from the viewpoint of the smallpox germ. The extermination of the smallpox germ could not have happened unless it was the Will of God according to the Cosmic Law; it is the exultation of the human being that exposes the fact that he tends to think of nothing but himself. That is the interpretation and arrogance of the split-mind of the human being, which is also the reason why he seeks happiness where no happiness can lie, and becomes frustrated and miserable. And, he will continue to be so until he recognizes himself as very much an integral part of the dream, of all nature, who cannot possibly be fundamentally superior to any other species of objects.

THE ULTIMATE UNDERSTANDING p. 155

I AM

The spontaneous arising of I Am (as a movement in Consciousness) is the sense of existence, the sense of presence. It brings about simultaneously and concurrently the appearance in consciousness of the phenomenal manifestation. The phenomenal manifestation necessitates *certain presupposed phenomenal conditions* without which such manifestation would not be possible. The wholeness and equanimity of the subjective noumenon (Consciousness-at-rest) gets apparently split into the duality of a pseudo-subject and an observed object. Each phenomenal sentient object then assumes subjectivity as a 'me' in reference to all other objects as 'others'. The objectification of this duality necessitates the apparent creation of the twin concepts of 'space' and 'time'. Space is necessary for the volume of objects to be extended. Time (duration) is necessary for the phenomenal images extended in space to be perceived, cognized and measured in terms of the duration of existence of each object and event.

THE FINAL TRUTH p. 15

What makes the seed sprout into its natural growth is Consciousness and nothing else. The first thought 'I Am' within the Consciousness creates the apparent diversity in manifestation. As space, Consciousness enables the seed to exist; as air, Consciousness breathes 'life' into it; as water, Consciousness nourishes it; while as earth, Consciousness provides the base for the seed to sprout. As light, Consciousness reveals its manifested form; while as sentience, Consciousness provides the means to perceive and cognize the manifested form. *Consciousness is all there is, expressing itself in various ways to bring about the manifestation and its functioning in totality.*

THE FINAL TRUTH p. 21

79

Bondage, to which the individual considers himself subject, is nothing but attachment to an illusory volition. It is attachment to a supposed 'will', which is to be translated as the exercise of an independent, personal choice of decision and action by that illusory entity with which What-One-Is is identified and which is called 'me'.

What this means is that the pronoun 'I' is used quite incorrectly. 'I' is, basically and fundamentally, the eternal subject without the slightest touch of objectivity. Yet, the pronoun is used for a phenomenal objectivization as if it were perfectly free to do whatever it wished, whenever and wherever it so wished. But the simple and incontrovertible fact is that an objectivization, like any other piece of a mechanism, can do nothing of itself.

What has in fact happened is that the driver of a motor car has identified himself with the car, and thereafter considers the car as 'me'. This assumed personality of the 'me-mechanism' is a concept, factually non-existent. This is what causes conflict, suffering and bondage. There is the need to function volitionally, as against the deepest intuitive conviction that the entity (supposed to exercise his volition) does not, cannot, exist.

THE FINAL TRUTH p. 55

When the incongruity of this situation is firmly understood, the illusion of a suffering entity in bondage, at once disappears. 'I' returns to its original subjectivity when the eclipse of the 'me' disappears. What lives (or, more correctly 'is lived') sensorially, is the object, and What-I-Am is its sentience. What-I-Am expresses itself as phenomenal functioning – seeing, hearing, tasting – but there is no objective 'I' (the 'me' is a fiction) that sees, hears, tastes. Only the object suffers and 'I' am not an object.

His *Sadguru* told him, 'If you dis-identify yourself from the body, and firmly remain entrenched in that animating consciousness which gives you sentience and the sense of presence – I AM – you will have peace and freedom from bondage this very instant'. And this is the 'knowledge' which he was now passing on to his listeners. Deep understanding and full conviction was all that is necessary. Any further action as such would indeed be not only not necessary but could actually prove to be a hindrance and obstruction.

EXPLORATIONS INTO THE ETERNAL p. viii

Hold on to the sense 'I am' to the exclusion of everything else. The mind being thus silent will shine with a new light and vibrate in the totality. When you keep the 'I am' feeling in the focus of awareness and watch yourself ceaselessly – *when there is continuous witnessing of all movements in consciousness* – the conscious and the unconscious will for a time play the game of hide-and-seek until finally the two become one and the one becomes the totality. The person then merges in the witness, the witness in awareness in pure Being – Who is there then to take a measure of that ecstasy?

EXPLORATIONS INTO THE ETERNAL p. 51

IDENTITY

The individual human body-mind mechanism is really nothing but an individual pattern of dynamic energy. That is all an individual is: energy vibrating and pulsating at an incredible speed in a particular pattern. And that pattern has characteristics peculiar to that particular body-mind organism. No human being has natural characteristics quite like any other.

THE BHAGAVAD GITA pp. 72–3

The absolutely basic concept is: the human being is, essentially, an object, a uniquely programmed instrument or computer, through which the Source or Primal Energy (or God) brings about such happenings, from moment to moment, as are supposed to happen according to a conceptual Cosmic Law, which the human being, as a mere created object, could never possibly understand.

THE ULTIMATE UNDERSTANDING p. 20

With the annihilation of the 'me-entity' comes peace and tranquility. There is no room for confusion or doubt or delusion. Concepts of heaven and hell, birth, death and rebirth, all get annihilated along with the 'me-entity'. What is more, even the delusion of liberation disappears together with that of bondage because both are based on the 'me' concept. And then it seems a miracle, not that the mind should be freed from the veil of ignorance, but that the mind should have been clouded and tainted by thought, percepts, concepts, desires and cravings in the first place.

THE FINAL TRUTH p. 230

I have so many 'selves' and while some of them may be 'good' – gentle, kind and noble, many others would be 'bad' – wild, cruel and obnoxious. Again, let me assure you, I am not being flippant. Actually the range of our 'selves' in this waking-dream is very much more inhibited than in our sleeping dreams. In our dreams we accept ourselves for whatever we appear to be, and it is only in retrospect that we judge ourselves according to the 'waking' standards.

Would not anything else be absurd? Whatever people think of me is *their* thought, visualized in their own aspect of the split-mind known as 'memory'. It is their mnemonic impression, which has nothing to do with me, with what I am or what I am not.

'Supposed to act'? How can an appearance be supposed to act? This was also told to us by the sages thousands of years ago, though of course in words and terms prevalent in their times. Therefore perhaps the need for books like this one. Anyway, the 'selves' do not 'act' – they *appear* to *react* to stimuli from outside, as images in mind.

This is the real trouble. Trying to put into words something that is indescribable turns it into a concept.

EXPERIENCING THE TEACHING pp. 67–8

Where there is neither being nor non-being, neither appearance nor void, neither subject nor object, there has, therefore, to be IDENTITY, which cannot perceive itself. That is non-conceptuality. That is subjectivity. That is absolute awareness not aware of itself. This is what we ARE. WHAT-WE-ARE cannot be the object of what-we-are.

EXPERIENCING THE TEACHING p. 57

Then there is the greater difficulty of the several conventional roles which every man has to adopt in the process of living in a community, apart from the fact that such communal living would necessarily involve an enormous amount of conditioning concerning law and order, ethics, conduct, etc. The difficulty operates at every step to such an extent that it is almost impossible to live one's life without a *personal identity* in some role or other – husband or wife, father or mother, white-collar worker or blue-collar worker – apart from the roles depending on a variety of hobbies. The result is that we are so accustomed – so deeply conditioned – to think in terms of an individual that it becomes almost impossible even to think in terms which do not include and involve the individual as a *separate entity* with autonomous choice of action.

The significance concerning a person's identity is twofold: one, that different people have different impressions based on past events, and the memories that these events have left in the brain as reactions to those events; two, these events and the reactions and memories relating to them are not all events but only a selection of events determined on the basis of standards that are not absolute standards but relative standards. In other words, conventions would necessarily be based on certain signs, symbols and measurements, with the result that conventional knowledge cannot but be a system of abstractions in which objects and events must necessarily be reduced to their general, hazy outlines. The astonishing but logical fact is that the individual entity thus turns out to be not only the 'metaphysical appearance in consciousness', but actually, and in everyday practical experience, *an abstract of general outlines based on certain selected impressions* concerning certain selected events. And it is from the point of view of such an individual entity that knowledge is sought. It is therefore not surprising that *knowledge that is not based on abstractions in which the individual entity becomes not only an irrelevance but an actual obstruction, is not easily apprehended.*

EXPLORATIONS INTO THE ETERNAL p. 204

It is important to realize that when the 'me-concept' sets itself up as the subjective reality, all that actually happens is that it considers itself an independent entity. It is not concerned with the rest of phenomenality and does not have any aggressive intention towards it; all it is concerned with is the protection and perpetual continuance of its own 'reality'. When there is conflict the 'me-concept' considers that it has been driven into this conflict by the 'other' which threatens its position! It is not concerned with victory over the adversary but merely wishes that the 'other' should let it remain in peace and happiness, and should therefore be driven away for good so that it would no longer threaten its security and well-being. All that the 'me-concept' is concerned with is that there should be no enemy to threaten its security. And the joke is that each 'me-concept' thinks exactly in terms of a separate independent entity – terms which are synonymous with dualism. The abandoning of polarity in the opposites means separation which brings about the fear of the 'other' and this fear manifests itself as human conflict and unhappiness.

EXPLORATIONS INTO THE ETERNAL p. 24

If the body is scientifically seen as emptiness, a throbbing energy, the question would arise: What then is a 'sentient being'? Perhaps the question answers itself. In the sentient being, if the *being* is merely emptiness, then the being that is sensorially perceptible must be a mere appearance like a mirage on the sands, and the 'sentient being' must be what remains: SENTIENCE. If the physical being is merely an appearance, an object, a phenomenon, it is quite obvious that it cannot be expected to perform any action as an independent entity on its own initiative. The fact is illustrated by the Chinese Master Chuan-tzu's oft-repeated story of the sow who died while her piglets were suckling – the little piglets just left the inanimate body because their mother was not there! The body became inanimate because the animus was no longer within. This animus, the sentience in the body, is regarded by the Eastern mystic as the consciousness (or the 'Heart' or the 'Mind') which is not the personal element in each sentient being but the universal, primal energy which pulsates in all sentient beings, and indeed in every particle in the entire universe. This impersonal or universal consciousness is, therefore, what the sentient being really is. And, indeed, all there is, all that exists, is nothing but the universal consciousness.

EXPLORATIONS INTO THE ETERNAL p. 15

Maharaj said a 'block' was an imaginary obstruction caused by an imaginary 'you', which had identified itself with the body. He said: 'I repeat, there must be a final and total negation so that the negator himself disappears! What you are trying to do is to understand what you are by means of a concept of 'existence', whereas in reality 'I' (you) *neither am, nor am not, 'I' am beyond the very concept of existence,* beyond the concept of both the positive and the negative presence. Unless this is understood very profoundly you will continue to create your own imaginary obstructions, each more powerful than the earlier one. *What you are trying to find is what you already are.*'

POINTERS FROM NISARGADATTA MAHARAJ p. 109

IGNORANCE

*A*vidya (ignorance) arises on *vidya* (knowledge) like ripples and waves arise on the surface of the ocean, and *avidya* dissolves in *vidya* just like the ripples and waves dissolve in the ocean. There is truly no difference between the waves and the water; similarly the distinction between ignorance and knowledge is notional and unreal. What exists, when ignorance and knowledge are no longer seen as two distinct entities, is Truth. The reflection of *vidya* within itself is considered *avidya* (ignorance), and when both these notions are abandoned, what remains is the Truth, phenomenally a void but noumenally the potential plenum or fullness. It is the reality in all things like the space within several pots. It causes cosmic movement and phenomenal manifestation without the slightest intention of doing so. It must, because that is its nature, just like a magnet makes iron filings move, merely by its presence.

What a horrendous thing this ignorance is. But it is really only like the second moon in diplopia. It creates an illusion in the mind. One thinks the shore is moving away when sitting in a moving boat. One thinks the train one is on is moving when actually the train is still and it is the other train that is moving away. Ignorance creates the living dream and perverts all experiences and relationships in dualism. And yet the moment there is realization of the real nature of the phenomenal manifestation – that it is really like the child of a barren woman – then ignorance is exposed and annihilated. When the flow of water ceases, the river dries up. *When dualism of ignorance ceases and conceptualization stops, there is phenomenal absence and noumenal presence.*

Once it is clearly understood that ignorance has no existence, that it is merely an illusion that has arisen as a movement in Consciousness, any further enquiries would be like projecting the future and examining the past of the child of a barren woman!

Ignorance vanishes as soon as it is examined critically. It is because of ignorance that one mistakes the silver in the mother-of-pearl. This ignorance can last only until the mother-of-pearl is seen for what it is. Ignorance vanishes as soon as it is apperceived that all that exists is the universal, infinite Consciousness. All phenomenal manifestations are merely appearances in Consciousness, like a mirror effect, and are therefore illusory. All that exists is Consciousness which can be represented by the personal subjective pronoun 'I'.

Ignorance not being a real entity, no relationship could possibly exist between ignorance and the Self. There can be relationship only between similar entities.

THE FINAL TRUTH pp. 184 & 207–8

INSECURITY

It is necessary to go to the root of the problem of insecurity in order to really understand it. And in the very understanding of the problem it disintegrates. The sense of security and the feeling of a need for it arise out of a misunderstanding of the basis of what we call life. The fact of the matter is that we do not really see that 'change' is an integral aspect of life. What we want is to stop the movie of life at a particular 'still', depending upon what that still means to us in terms of what we *then* consider as happiness. When we fail to see *change as life itself*, just as the flow is really the river, we become like Ouroboros, the misguided snake, who tries to eat his own tail. The only way to make sense out of change is to join it. You cannot avoid it! There is no other way. Either plunge into life and welcome change as the spice of life or resist and set yourself against yourself.

The root of the frustration which the civilized man feels today lies in the fact that he lives not for the present moment but for the illusory future, the future which is only a creation of brain and therefore a mere inference based on memory, an abstraction at best. It is the brain, or the divided or split mind, which creates the future whereas the *whole* mind knows no future for the simple reason that it does not conceptualize and lives totally in the present reality. The whole mind knows only 'What-Is' whereas the split-mind, working through the brain and its memory, has created a 'present future' which has a high degree of accuracy only in so far as the ponderables are concerned. For example, everyone will grow old and will need an income in the absence of the ability to work, everyone will die, etc. However, the split-mind cannot handle imponderables.

It is clear that the brain, with its fantastic memory bank, is an absolute necessity in order to live in this world. But the trouble is that the individual mind is a split or divided mind and we cannot ignore the whole mind because the whole mind is the *basic* universal

Consciousness. Indeed most physical processes concerning breathing, swallowing, digesting, circulating of blood, etc. are extraordinarily complex processes with which the brain has little to do. These processes are called 'involuntary' and brushed aside as of little consequence. This is where the root of the whole trouble lies – the dichotomy created in the modern man between his brain (the cortex) and the rest of his body, between the whole mind and the split-mind, between the 'I' and 'me', between the impersonal or universal Consciousness and the personal consciousness identified with the separate psychosomatic apparatus. In other words, we need both the brain-thinking and the instinctive wisdom to lead a harmonious and well-balanced life, but what we have done is to allow the brain-thinking to develop so quickly and so fast that we have almost forgotten all about the instinctive wisdom which has thereby nearly slumped into atrophy.

What man wants is security for the future. He cannot really be happy even if the present moment provides him with everything that his heart desires. He must have a future he can look forward to, and his experience of the past tells him that 'security' has never had anything resembling permanency. It is clear to him that even if he does achieve his goal at some time in the future, the 'future' does not stop with the achievement of that particular goal. What he is chasing is actually nothing better than a will-o'-the-wisp. The real tragedy of this situation is that he cannot even enjoy that which is available to him at the present moment in a large measure. But when there is true understanding, there is acceptance of the present moment – and whatever it offers – which permits a total, uninhibited enjoyment of it. It is this fact which describes the *jnani* (one who is established in Truth) as *mahabhokta*, the supreme enjoyer.

THE FINAL TRUTH pp. 153, 155 & 217–18

THE JNANI

The seedlings of sugar cane do not look like sugar cane, but they are pregnant with juice. The full moon is full of its brilliance which thereafter does not wane.

The moonlight falls also on the moon; the rain falls on the sea. But the moon and the sea are not affected thereby. This is the way the senses of the self-realized man meet sense objects.

AMRITANUBHAVA BY JNANESHWAR

The seedlings of sugar cane do not yearn to grow into sugar cane; they are already pregnant with the juice. And the full moon is already full of radiance and does not hanker after more. Falling of water into the sea as the rains does not satisfy any desire on the part of the sea for more water. The moon has all the brilliance it needs or wants, and the sea has all the water it needs or desires. Therefore, when moonlight falls on the moon or more water is fed into the sea, the moon and the sea are indifferent. Jnaneshwar says that this is the way the sense organs of the *Jnani* meet sense objects. The *Jnani* is indifferent. He does not hanker after more pleasures nor does he refuse whatever comes his way by way of sense objects. Wanting something positively or not wanting anything negatively are both aspects of volition. In the case of the *Jnani* there is no volition, either positive or negative. The absence of volition comports the absence of identification with any separate entity because such identification is the very basis of volition. If there is no separate entity, who or what will choose and want something and strive for it? In other words, the *Jnani* has apperceived the fact that all interrelated opposites such as likes and dislikes,

91

love and hate are conceptual and are the cause of the conceptual bondage; and this apperceiving itself is the liberation from the concept of bondage. Such apperceiving is the state of non-being, non-identity – the identified man gets involved, the non-identified watches the show as a witness.

EXPERIENCE OF IMMORTALITY pp. 206–7

For the awakened there is no question of making any choice. All actions HAPPEN as part of the functioning of Totality – there is no question of the wise man making any choice or decision: all actions are intuitive, and he does not even think of the propriety or otherwise of the actions that have happened. It is for this reason that he is sometimes misunderstood as being insensitive to the feelings of others: no individual exists who could be either sensitive or insensitive – but deep down what exists is COMPASSION, otherwise he would not bother to talk.

CONSCIOUSNESS WRITES p. 32

What the sage is saying in these verses is that what characterizes the 'wise man', the 'rare one', the 'great soul' is the fact that he lives in this world as if he is not in it. In other words, he lives in this world as if he is acting a role in a dream-play. The sense objects no longer attract him. Experiences do not leave any impression on him. He neither craves for sensual gratification nor hankers after spiritual awakening. He is indifferent to the various motivations in life – dharma, artha, kama, moksha. He is in fact not even concerned whether he lives or dies.

A DUET OF ONE p. 132

A true sage would rather not be known as a sage.

THE ULTIMATE UNDERSTANDING p. 24

The yogi – the *jnani* – is not particularly elated because he is established in his natural state, the noumenal state that transcends all pain and pleasure which are phenomenal experiences. Indeed, what Janaka points out is that all the pitfalls, which Ashtavakra has so very compassionately indicated, have all been transcended. They cannot affect him any more because he is fully aware that all phenomenal objects are mere appearances, concepts which have no nature of their own. He also brings out the fact that Indra and the other gods are only conceptual creations, and an object (a concept) cannot be enlightened, whether he is a sentient being or a god.

The *jnani* is not affected by the operations of the interrelated opposites like virtue and vice which are only phenomenal concepts because he is not involved with any actions which might take place through 'his' psychosomatic organism. There is only witnessing. The sky of the *jnani*'s witnessing is not affected by the smoke and pollution of the phenomenal actions that are taking place as part of the functioning of totality. Phenomenal actions can affect only an object through the consequences, but when the 'me' has been totally demolished, the 'I' forever transcends all phenomenality. In an indirect, respectful way, Janaka is assuring his guru with supreme confidence that the ego has indeed been annihilated.

'Acting as he wishes' clearly means spontaneous actions for the simple reason that the *jnani* has no will or volition of his own. Therefore, all actions which appear to be those of an individual are, in reality, the spontaneous activity of the noumenal functioning. In this verse, Janaka brings out the fact that although some actions of 'his' might *appear* to have the taint of not conforming to scriptural injunctions, they are not the actions of an identified individual with supposed volition. As such, they are totally impersonal without the slightest touch of doership. In other words, all activity, appearing to be performed by the *jnani*, is spontaneous noumenal activity *of that moment*. It is merely witnessed by the *jnani*, without any involvement, without any judging. If someone has been helped, it is not because of his wish. If someone has not been helped, it is not in spite of his wish!

The *jnani* lives only in the present moment, not concerned with duration.

A DUET OF ONE p. 62

The circle is completed, the *Jnani* continues his phenomenal existence till the end of his allotted span in perfect adaptation to whatever might happen, without losing his inherent sense of equanimity. His living then is non-volitional living. He lives in the conceptual present moment, he neither thinks of the past (whether painful or pleasurable) nor of the future (with hope or fear). Thus while the past and the future are based on volition and wish fulfillment, presence in the HERE AND NOW is eternal because there is no individual who can know it phenomenally. The *Jnani*'s 'being present in the present' is *phenomenally* non-volitional living; *noumenally* it is being in the intemporality of the awakened state. Therefore, the life of a *Jnani* appears to others to be purposeless. In the words of a Zenrin poem:

The wild geese do not intend to cast their reflection;
The water has no mind to receive their image.

There is a very beautiful verse in the *Ashtavakra Gita*, the purport of which is: 'The spontaneous unrestrained outburst from a *Jnani* is a glorious thing free as it is from motivation and preference, but not the unnatural and assumed quietude of the hypocrite who is still attached to his individual identity.'

There is futility in trying to see – and judge – a *Jnani* by relative norms and through the viewpoint of a split-mind which the common man usually does. He used to say that the perceived is a mirror in which the perceiver sees his own image.

Ramana Maharshi too was averse to answering questions about the relative state of the *Jnani* and positively discouraged such questions. He would sometimes quote a verse from Bhagavata which says: 'Just as an intoxicated person is not aware whether his upper garment is on his body or has slipped off the body, similarly the *Jnani* is only dimly

conscious of his body and is totally indifferent whether the body exists
or not.'

The essential significance of the analysis would seem to be to bring out
the fact it would be futile to try to form a distinct image of the *Jnani*,
that it is only a Jnani who would recognize another *Jnani*.

EXPLORATIONS INTO THE ETERNAL pp. 105, 56, 53 & 61

He who cannot give up the will to make an effort cannot hope for
enlightenment even if Shiva offers to be his Guru. Similar is the case
of the one who cannot give up his skepticism towards the Guru's
guidance. On the other hand, the one who is disturbed only by desires
as such will reach the goal even though with some difficulty, and after
some time and effort will be able to remain absorbed in the consciousness. He belongs to the middle class, in the classification of
sages, as a sage without mind.

The lowest among the sages are those whose psychic predispositions
have not been destroyed. They are still concerned with their thoughts
and are on the borderline of being *Jnanis*. They appear to share
pleasures and pains of life like an ordinary individual and will be
emancipated only after death.

Chapter XX (116–33) of *Tripura Rahasya* makes another distinction
among the sages: 'Some sages abide in consciousness even while they
are engaged in their normal duties; others can do so only when they
are not otherwise engaged; still others can do so only at specific times
by constant practice. These are the respective levels in a descending
order.

'He is the perfect sage who, though engaged in work, does not
consider anyone or anything as other than the self; who while doing
his work efficiently remains as if he is asleep; who, whether he is
working or not, is for all purposes never out of Samadhi; who from his
own experience is capable of recognizing the state of other *Jnanis*; who
realizes pleasure, pain and all other phenomena to be mere movements
in consciousness, and feels himself pervading the entire manifestation. He is the perfect sage who, knowing the trammels of bondage

(to be merely a concept), *does not care to seek emancipation and remains perfectly contented* (in the totality of the functioning of manifestation).'

Chapter XXI says something more on the subject. Thus it is said (25–9): 'What comes to others as accomplishments through dispassion, meditation, prayers, etc. seems an integral part of his psyche, and comes naturally to the perfect sage, on whom neither praise nor insult, neither loss nor gain has any effect. He can give spontaneous answers (which have the stamp of truth) in matters pertaining to the highest truth and enlightenment and is never tired of talking about such matters (to the sincere seeker). He is totally relaxed without effort and perfectly contented in any situation.'

EXPLORATIONS INTO THE ETERNAL p. 60

JOY

What happens in moments of sheer joy or pleasure? We have no difficulty in being the experience of the moment by forgetting 'ourselves' (the 'me' is absent and there is only the joy of the experience). The mind remains whole and is not divided from the experience. The problem arises only when there is pain whether actual or imagined, and then the vicious circle of the split mind begins its course, with the effort of the 'me' to escape from the pain and the consequent tension. A conscious relaxation of the entire body-mind releases the tension – and the pain – to an astonishing extent. This conscious relaxation is the outcome of the awareness of the fear itself, together with the realization that tension can only make the pain worse. The fear is really based on *the memory* of past experiences and not on the past experiences themselves because those are dead. The relaxation is an expression of the willingness to welcome the new experience without any mental resistance or reservation.

What the ultimate understanding brings about is joy deep in the heart of one's being. Such joy is pure joy. It treats alike all experiences of pleasure and misery that might appear momentarily on the surface. Such pure joy, which is like the ultimate understanding, is denoted by the traditional term *Sat-chit-ananda* (existence-consciousness-bliss), the very essence of the source of all manifestation.

When understanding takes place there may not be an irrepressible cascading of joy. Thus, when enlightenment took place, the Buddha, it is said, sat for seven days in total silence. He thought: 'Those who are destined to understand will understand even if I do not utter a word; those who are destined not to understand will not understand even if I talk incessantly; those who are destined to understand will understand through some word or some event howsoever insignificant; those who are about to awaken from sleep will awaken even

97

through the softest sound or even the gentlest breeze, while others may not awaken even if they are roughly shaken.' It is said that the great Chinese sage Lao Tzu received sudden enlightenment when he was sitting under a tree and saw a dry leaf fall from a branch of the tree. The dry leaf became his guru.

THE FINAL TRUTH pp. 158 & 210

LETTING GO

There is a more subtle aspect of this matter of 'giving-up' (or 'letting go'). There is one kind of giving up which has, as its basis, the giving up of one thing in order to get something later. But there is a more genuine giving up where something is given up as being harmful or useless, by itself, not necessarily in exchange for something more acceptable. It is a question of giving up a concept or an illusion out of a conviction about its illusoriness, without any other motive. What the sage is saying is not that giving up the separation between 'me' and the 'other' will bring about happiness, but simply that when this illusory separation is lost what remains *is* happiness. In other words, the original state of oneness is happiness, and that separation is a sort of eclipse of that state. With the end of separation, the original state of happiness prevails in its pristine state. It is not a question of giving up a smaller house in order to buy a bigger house!

A DUET OF ONE pp. 113 & 14

LIBERATION

What the sage says between the lines in this chapter is that since what-we-are, by its very nature, is absolutely free and totally unconditioned, any concept of – and, along with it, any desire for – liberation and the personal achieving of enlightenment is in itself an impediment to the impersonal apperception of that freedom. In any case, such apperception cannot be an object perceivable by a perceiver. There can only be the perceiving which itself is the Truth. In trying to apprehend Reality, the error that clouds all understanding is that an attempt is made to understand that-which-we-are (the Reality) on an objective basis whilst Reality is pure subjectivity, the only subject without the slightest objective quality. Indeed Reality is that on which appears the temporal manifestation of phenomena which are mistakenly considered by the sentient objects as 'real'.

EXPERIENCE OF IMMORTALITY p. 90

LIFE

In the sleeping-dream, when the dreamer awakes, the dream-ing ends, and there is no question of what is happening to the other 'beings' or phenomena in the dream. The same thing happens in the living-dream, but there is a difficulty in seeing that there are no 'beings' but only phenomena inasmuch as we continue to be participants in the living dream. And, therefore, it is not easy to accept that all 'beings', *including ourselves*, are merely illusory phenomena.

Living is a movie on the screen of 'space', an illusion of movement created by the serializing of the three-dimensional 'stills', perceived and cognized only so long as the light of consciousness is available. Once the light of consciousness is off, the screen of space, the three-dimensional characters and the events on the screen disappear. The movie no longer functions – this is called 'dying'.

THE ULTIMATE UNDERSTANDING pp. 210 & 211

'I' am the subjective Reality, the dreamer of myself in the Cosmic dream in which I appear. I cannot therefore possibly be the objective, dreamed appearance and, therefore, too, I am not an entity. It is never the object that awakens, only the dreamer who awakens from the iden-tification with the dreamed object that is the cause of the illusion of bondage. 'Awakening' in effect, means vanishing as a dreamed object, the dissolving of appearance, the evaporation of the illusion or dream. Awakening therefore amounts to the discovery that the apparent entity has disappeared along with the total illusion or dream. The dreamed object is, in fact and substance, nothing other than the subjective Reality, now uncovered by the disappearance of the illusion.

THE FINAL TRUTH p. 24

As a matter of fact, we are indeed being lived in what the sage Vasishtha asseverates to be the living dream, in which volition cannot possibly have any role to play. The sage makes it very clear (in the *Yogavasishtha*) that life in its seriality is a dream similar in every respect to the personal dream. Volition, therefore, is only an imagined and not actual factor in our lives. Non-volition, therefore means the abandoning of volitional action, not through the apparent volition of the illusory ego that appears to function and 'do' things, but as the result or consequence of the understanding itself, the understanding that is the dis-identification with the illusory ego and an identification, *though notional*, with WHAT-WE-ARE. Such understanding, that Maharaj referred to, leaves the mind vacant or fasting so that it can receive the intuitional apprehension which automatically results in the totality of functioning, in which the ego can have no relevance.

Such intuitive understanding – the apperception – resulting in noumenal activity means *experiencing* the Teaching.

No. Awakening means realizing that what is apparently objective is truly subjective. The dreamed-object cannot be anything other than its source; the dreamer, the consciousness, that is dreaming. The point is that the dreamed-objects cannot have any nature of their own other than that of their source. The shadow has no nature of its own other than that of the substance without which the shadow cannot occur.

During the continuation of the life span, the dreamed character – the dreamer – exists only as an object in the living dream of 'others' who are as yet unawakened. The awakened knows that 'he' himself is the awakening. There is the apperception that he is the pure unconditioned subjectivity by means of which he and all sentient beings were dreamed. In fact, the dreamer, on awakening, finds that there never was a dreamer, only the phenomenon of dreaming.

EXPERIENCING THE TEACHING pp. 104, 44 & 46

All that man can do is to forget his individual separateness and witness the functioning of the Totality, as in a dream. And, truly, even this is not in his hands as an individual, but becomes a part of the totality of functioning, which, ironically is his own objective expression, not as an individual object 'me' but as the Absolute Subject, what Ramana Maharshi called the 'I-I', the throbbing formless beingness or presence.

EXPLORATIONS INTO THE ETERNAL p. 246

An important point is that a clear understanding of 'what is' does not make us shut out the phenomenal world as an illusion because then we would be making a false distinction between the real and the unreal, between the substance and the shadow, between the noumenon and the phenomenon. All there is is reality, and any illusion, any appearance, any shadow cannot but be a reflection of that very reality. To consider that the phenomenal universe, being an illusion, is other than reality would mean that we are making reality something less than the totality it is. The true understanding accepts the position that noumenality is at once both transcendent to and immanent in phenomenality, and, therefore, all distinctions are seen to be void. In other words, nothing is seen as acceptable or not acceptable, existing or not existing, with the result that dispassion is cultivated through the realization that neither the attractive nor the unattractive attributes of things have any absolute existence. And, most important, rivalry in the world becomes a game – a *Lila* – rather than a strife and conflict. In short, the immediate result of the deep understanding is that *man frees himself from the world and its ills and sufferings and chaos by seeing the absurdity of it*. He sees that what he had considered and labelled as desirable or undesirable, and based his ideals and aims in life on, such illusory distinctions, merely constitute the diversity in the course of life which otherwise would have been an unbearable bore. An apperception of the basic meaninglessness of conventional values in terms of reality lifts man out of the apparent strife and conflict of life so that he now sees it as a game in which he must participate according to the rules but which he need not at all take seriously. How does this happen? The man who has, through the understanding of 'what is', freed himself from conventional standards of judgement, considers it stupid either to accept the suffering that is imposed by those very standards, or at the same time to immerse himself in what are usually considered great joys. He does not in any literal sense withdraw and hide himself from the material world of people and events, for to do so would at once mean a confession of having passed a judgement upon the world based on the same conventional values. He continues to remain within society but refrains from acting out of the prevailing motives that make the ordinary man struggle for wealth, fame and security, the very same motives and intentions which create the karma for the individual. Cheerfully accepting whatever comes his way, without any judgement, as part of the totality of functioning, he remains within the underlying unity that encompasses man and nature in the totality that is the universe, and wanders through life enjoying all experiences without ever becoming attached – either positively to the delights or negatively to the sorrows – in any way.

For the *Lila* of 'Life' as such, there must be a script and the script must bring in causes which lead to certain effects which in turn would become causes for yet further effects in future, and such causes and effects must, of course, function through individuals as the characters in the life's drama. But then in these circumstances the various individuals as characters in the drama of life merely perform their roles and then disappear. Where is the question of the one individual (*jiva*) going through various characters at various times, each new character being based on the facts of his 'independent' actions in his life as the previous character? Does the individual really have such independence and autonomy in each of his lives? This is an interesting and intriguing aspect of the phenomena of life and death when considered in the space-time duality in which the universe manifests itself.

EXPLORATIONS INTO THE ETERNAL pp. 165 & 195

I may believe that the whole universe is a dream and all human beings are characters within that dream, but so long as one remains outside the dream and sees it as something seen by him as a separate entity, he cannot be any nearer to liberation or Self-realization. 'Liberation' is nothing other than the liberation from this idea of a separate entity doing the seeing.

It is only when the 'me' is included in the dreamed universe, and the apperception, as such, does not include a separate 'me' to do the perceiving, that the phenomenal 'me' vacates the position for the noumenal 'I' to come in – the 'I' who is the dreamer and the dreaming, the seeker and the sought.

THE ULTIMATE UNDERSTANDING p. 192

LISTENING

When the listening is done by the individual, it is the mind-intellect that does the listening and it is of the nature of conceptualizing. When the listening is done by Consciousness, the individual is absent in such listening and then it is of the nature of EXPERIENCING. In other words, while intellectual listening is 'considering the Teaching', listening without the individual present is 'EXPERIENCING the Teaching'.

Intellectual listening is done by the individual who in fact is merely an image in the mind. What this amounts to is perceiving *this* that is objectivized, and such perceiving prevents the apperceiving of *that* WHICH-IS. When the individual ('me'-concept) is absent in the listening with the whole mind, the separation between the listener and the listening is lost. The listening then becomes part of the totality of functioning without any interference from the split mind. Then the Guru's words hit the target like an arrow because the path of the arrow was not blocked by the 'me'-concept.

Mere hearing by the ears is not enough, there must be listening by the mind and the heart. The repeated complaints from people that they seem to comprehend the Teaching at some point of time but they lose it 'thereafter'. The point is that even if we could remove the notion of 'me' for a moment and we do this quite often – its enduring in time remains, and it comes back again and again. We cannot destroy our 'me'-ness without destroying its duration – the two concepts are inseparable, two aspects of the same notion.

The listener should a) read the *Bhagavad Gita* from Lord Krishna's point of view, and b) try to go behind the words that He uttered.

The point was that the listening should be done with a receptive mind; an aggressively critical mind would erect a barrier between the spoken word and the listened word. In other words, there should be an honesty of intent in listening, so that the attention is not on the apparent contradiction but in the real meaning behind the apparent contradiction.

EXPERIENCING THE TEACHING pp. 31, 81 & 130

The sound dies, but that which hears remains; leave sound to itself and hear the hearing instead.

THE ULTIMATE UNDERSTANDING p. 32

Would it mean anything to you if I said that you have come here to listen to me, but you must listen to me on the basis that this 'you' is wholly illusory, that there is really no 'you' who could listen to my words and get any benefit! Indeed, I must go so far as to say that unless you give up your role of an individual listener expecting some benefit out of what you hear, words for you would be mere empty sounds. The obstruction preventing apperception is that although you might prepare yourself to accept the thesis that everything in the universe is illusory, in this illusoriness you fail to include yourself! Now, do you see the problem – or is it more a joke than a problem?

When – let me not say 'if' – you accept this basis for your listening, that is to say, you give up all concern for the listener wanting to be a 'better' individual by listening to the words and hoping to 'work' towards a perceptible improvement, then do you know what would happen? Then, in that state of intuitive listening, *when the 'listener' no longer intrudes*, words would throw up and expose their subtle, inner meaning, which the 'fasting' or open mind will grasp and apperceive with deep and instant conviction. And then will words have achieved even their limited fulfillment!

When the listener remains in a state of suspension without intruding on the listening as such, what in fact happens is that the relative, divided mind is automatically restrained from its natural proclivity to engage itself in tortuous interpretation of words, and is thereby prevented from maintaining a continuous process of objectification. It is then the whole mind that is enabled to be in direct communion with both the talking and the listening as such, and thereby to bring about the Yoga of words, enabling the words to yield their innermost meaning and their most subtle significance.

POINTERS FROM NISARGADATTA MAHARAJ p. 158

LOVE

There is yet another aspect of Shiva and Shakti swallowing each other. Nisargadatta Maharaj gave considerable importance to it. To the question why consciousness arose at all in that state of unicity when awareness was not aware of itself – why consciousness went into a state of movement from its position of rest – Maharaj's answer was that consciousness throbbed itself into existence spontaneously because it is its nature to do so. This 'nature' is LOVE and any expression of love needs duality. The sea creates clouds out of itself and then accepts the clouds back into itself as the rains – and this is a continuous phenomenon. This is the sort of thing that happens when consciousness erupts into movement and merges itself again into awareness, which is consciousness at rest. It is again necessary to state that the two are not in essence separate. This sense of LOVE, which consciousness is in essence, gets turned into love for the material objects of the world when consciousness identifies itself with objects through which it manifests itself. This is Maya.

Our real nature is pure LOVE which must return to its source, the pure awareness. This pure love, our true nature, we have forgotten through the power of Maya, and have replaced it by our attachment for material objects – love for certain objects and hate for others, both interrelated opposites in duality. When, by the grace of the Guru, there is apperception of the truth, love for material objects naturally and smoothly gets itself converted into pure LOVE. Thus LOVE and love – Shiva and Shakti – get converted into each other first through Maya and then back through self-realization; they swallow each other and never let anything interfere with their basic unity.

EXPERIENCE OF IMMORTALITY, pp. 7–8

It is this feeling of LOVE *that arises* which holds the universe together – it is a spontaneous arising, totally independent of the 'instruction' to love thy neighbor. LOVE is not made to order!

CONSCIOUSNESS WRITES p. 47

'True' love can only mean the absence of separation. When there is the deepest apprehension that all human beings are merely uniquely programmed instruments through which the Impersonal Energy functions by way of actions – and, therefore, there cannot be any individual doer of actions – only then will there be an absence of separation which could be termed 'love' or 'universal love', but which is in fact more accurately termed 'harmony' or 'beatitude'.

Love is one of those words which have caused, over the centuries, a considerable amount of confusion, because of which, perhaps, the world is amended to 'universal love' or even 'divine love'. But the fact remains that what is sought to be conveyed by the word 'love' is essentially a personally experienced emotion, which, deeply entrenched in a possessiveness that is closely interlinked with jealousy, cannot keep 'love' very far from its interconnected opposite, 'hate'. Sages cannot know this love-hate relationship, an affectivity corrupted by the perpetual egoism, the sense of personal doership.

Love is wanting to do something for the other without the slightest expectation of anything in return.

THE ULTIMATE UNDERSTANDING pp. 188, 119 & 44

In the beginning, the love for the Guru cannot but be intensely personal, but as the understanding gets deeper, his love continues on a personal level but is based deeper down on the impersonal love for the Guru as Consciousness.

This is where the 'Guru' comes into the picture – but *not* as the teacher or the counselor or the guide, in the sense the Westerner thinks of 'the person'. Frankly wherever there has occurred a real transformation – not merely an intellectual understanding – I have clearly seen a very distinct transformation in the understanding of the Guru-disciple relationship. LOVE arises for the Guru in a torrent of emotion which thereafter becomes the substratum of all future understanding that ultimately ends in apperception – the disappearance of the fear of all phenomenal problems, resulting in a perpetual feeling of total freedom, a feeling of lightness, of floating in the air, 'like a dry leaf in the breeze'. This transformation is NOT phenomenal: it is a different dimension brought about by the deepest feeling of reverence for the Guru. Needless to say, this is an occurrence over which no individual has any kind of volition or control.

Almost invariably, this overpowering feeling results in copious tears, because this feeling is the realization that the Guru is not separate from the disciple, that both are the SELF that is being sought!

And always, to the Guru all relationships are nothing but impersonal happenings.

CONSCIOUSNESS WRITES pp. 17 & 18

Finally, it must be admitted that the basic teaching does not include any abstract theory of 'universal love'. This is so because LOVE is not something apart from the Understanding. The oft-preached 'universal love' is based on the premise that the individual must find his own happiness in caring for the common good of all. This makes such an inordinate demand on the human nature that when pursued to an extreme it will only lead to very deep frustration. Indeed, love and compassion are something natural to man when he is not conditioned by the self-motive, but when pursued through a constructed system that ignores the fundamental realities, such pursuit must inevitably turn love into hate.

The final understanding is that Love is all there is.

RIPPLES p. 44

'Love' – as the word is generally understood – denotes separation, whereas a non-objective relationship means not 'lover' but 'compassion' or *karuna*. The essence of this is immediate joy, being at-one-ment. We do not 'love' others, we *are* others.

A DUET OF ONE p. 48

Now, let us go back again to what I told you about need being the basis of love. Consider what is the most priceless possession of any sentient being. If he had the choice of possessing either all the wealth in the world or his 'beingness', or 'consciousness' (you may give it any name to add to the thousands that have already been heaped upon it), that which gives him the sense of being alive and present, and without which the body would be nothing but a cadaver, what would he choose? Obviously, without consciousness, all the wealth in the world would be of no use to him. This beingness, this conscious presence that he is, is the beingness of every sentient being on the earth, the very soul of the entire universe – and indeed, therefore, *this-here-now, this conscious presence, cannot be anything other than God.* It is this which one loves more than anything else because without it there is no universe, no God. This, therefore, is *Presence-Love-God.* And, St John was obviously very much conscious of this when he said 'God is Love ...! It is very clear that all he could have meant is that he (John) and He (God) were not different as pure subjectivity, as noumenon. And, therefore, he who is anchored in the conscious presence that is Love, that is God, 'dwelleth in God and God in him'.

POINTERS FROM NISARGADATTA MAHARAJ p. 116

The spontaneous 'Love' feeling that came over you was indeed the deepest dip into I-Am-ness that we all are, the *total* disappearance – momentary though it might have been – of the individual 'me' which has superimposed itself on this fundamental primal state of Consciousness, which is indeed Love or Compassion, the sudden real-ization of which brings tears to one's eyes. This is a 'dip' deeper into the love relationship between the guru and the disciple which is a prevailing condition *in phenomenality*, a dip into the solution of continuity between phenomenality and noumenality.

Love, the objective expression of the absolute subject: Love Of Oneself as Unicity.

How does this Love express itself phenomenally? It is on this point that there is some misconception regarding such expression of Love (or Compassion) by Totality through body-mind organisms in which enlightenment has occurred. What really happens is that whatever the acts that take place through the concerned body-mind mechanism, the pervading understanding is that *it does not matter* to the particular body-mind mechanism in the absence of the 'me'. Of course, some of these acts could raise doubts in the minds of others (not 'others' to the *jnani*) until understanding happens, but the *jnani* is not concerned with such reactions just as the ordinary man, on waking up, is not concerned with the actions and reactions of the characters in the dream.

In other words, the awakening brings about the depth of the ocean. It does not necessarily stop the arising of the waves and the froth.

CONSCIOUSNESS TO CONSCIOUSNESS pp. 83 & 72

MEDITATION

Meditation, which means 'sitting thinking' or 'sitting thinking of not thinking', necessarily requires a 'me'-entity doing the meditation. Meditation, done with a determination over a certain period, will almost certainly produce some 'results', some kinds of experiences, which would encourage the meditator because of the progress thus made. But these results or experiences can only be at the conceptual level. The danger is that, instead of the vital purpose of the demolition of the 'me'-entity with volition, the progress might actually strengthen the ego-entity: the progress might continually produce more and more expectation, more and more testing of the progress by the ego-doer.

The aim is the dis-appearance of the conceptual appearance of the ego-entity which impedes the apprehension of what-we-are. This can come about only when there is no 'me'-entity as the volitional doer of the meditation, expecting a certain result as quickly as possible. Therefore, true meditation is that meditation which happens when there is no meditator to evaluate the results of the meditation.

THE ULTIMATE UNDERSTANDING p. 181

The word 'meditate' is used precisely to denote the 'non-action' that could produce the awakening to enlightenment. Ashtavakra urges his disciple to realize his identity as the non-dual Consciousness and to remain in that realization in which the split-mind is totally absent. In such meditation, there is no ego present as the meditator. There is only the realization of the identity as the non-dual Consciousness.

When Ashtavakra says in verse 15 that practicing meditation is the very bondage from which liberation is sought, the meaning is clear that such meditation presupposes the deliberate action of the ego as the meditator, practicing meditation, with the specific intention of realizing something. And whatever the ego does is creating further cords of bondage. The point is simple. The basic Truth is that the true nature of all sentient beings is pure Consciousness which is the substance of all phenomenal appearances. If this is accepted – and it must be – then anyone wanting to 'do' something, in order to 'become' enlightened, is surely turning his back on the basic Truth.

Janaka then proceeds to the matter of meditation. He says that he finds no need for any action including meditation because that would presuppose the acquisition of something, even though it be the holy object of achieving liberation. He makes the bold statement that he finds all such methods and efforts to be distractions and that instead he simply abides in his natural state. When he abides in that natural state, all interdependent opposites negate each other and disappear completely and there is nothing to be accepted or rejected. Even thinking about the unthinkable is an exercise in futility. All that is necessary, says Janaka, is to abide in one's real nature.

In the next eight verses Janaka concludes by exclaiming how truly simple it is to give up all effort and thereby negate the conceptual do-er who is the villain. And then there is nothing to attain, nothing to achieve. One is home!

A DUET OF ONE pp. 30 & 88

NOUMENON*

'Phenomena' and 'noumenon' might be said to be two aspects of non-conceptuality. Noumenon, as the source of everything, cannot be anything; and a phenomenon, being devoid of self-nature is no thing in itself but, as the emanation from noumenon, is everything. A deep understanding that neither can be anything but that everything is both – that forever separate as concepts, they are, when unconceived, eternally inseparable – is the experiencing of the Teaching. Indeed, that identity is itself this experience.

EXPERIENCING THE TEACHING p. 56

Noumenon – pure subjectivity – is not aware of its existence. Such awareness of its existence comes about only with the arising of consciousness – I am. This spontaneous arising of consciousness (because that is its nature, as Maharaj said) brings about the sense of presence, of existence. Simultaneously, it causes the arising of the phenomenal manifestation in consciousness, together with a sense of duality. The Wholeness gets split into the duality of a (pseudo) subject and observed object – each phenomenal object assumes subjectivity as a 'me' concerning all other objects as 'others'. The objectivization of this duality requires the creation of the twin concepts of 'space' and 'time': 'space' in which the volume of objects could be extended, and 'time' in which the phenomenal images extended in space could be perceived, cognized and measured in terms of the duration of existence.

*A word widely used by the great philosopher Immanuel Kant. Kant refers to the distinction between phenomenon and noumenon as one of the most important distinctions in philosophy. The distinction is between the apparent world of sensible phenomena and the intelligible invisible world of Reality. [Ed.]

What-we-are, as noumenon, is intemporal, infinite, imperceptible being. What-we-appear-to-be as phenomena, is temporal, finite, sensorially perceptible separate object. Truly, we are illusory figments in consciousness. The fact that we, as separate, illusory entities, absurdly expect to be able to transform ourselves into enlightened beings, shows the extent of the conditioning to which we have been subjected. How can a phenomenon, a mere appearance, perfect itself? Only dis-identification with the supposed entity can bring about the transformation.

Speaking as 'I' (noumenon), we can all – each one of us – say to our phenomenal selves, 'be still and know that I am God.' It is only when the phenomenal self is absent that the noumenal 'I' can be present.

Noumenality cannot include any concepts. What every seeker truly seeks – all do not realize it – is the absence of both the positive and the negative aspects of entity. But so long as there is any seeking – and thus the seeker – the absence of what is present as an entity (positive or negative) cannot happen. A self-anchored phenomenal object cannot possibly find the noumenon that it truly is, just as it is impossible for a shadow to find its substance. The apparent seeker in space-time is a concept. What is sought is another concept. So is the seeking and the finding (or non-finding). The absolute absence of all such concepts means the abandoning of the quest and such abandoning results in the annihilation of the seeker into BEINGNESS.

EXPERIENCING THE TEACHING pp. ix–xii & 88

NOW

At any moment, whatever is manifest is perfect. If this is deeply understood, every moment is welcomed and whatever that moment brings – 'good' or 'not good' – is accepted without any judgement, without expectation or anxiety. It is this attitude of acceptance which is the real freedom, freedom from expectation and desire, freedom from fear and anxiety. When this is deeply understood, you do not bother about what happens, what thoughts occur or what actions take place, or what emotions arise – they are all witnessed.

CONSCIOUSNESS WRITES p. 11

Ashtavakra finally concludes that when the being itself is centered in the here-and-now, the body-mind apparatus may live anywhere for the simple reason that the body-mind apparatus, freed from the desire and volition of the 'me', becomes the vehicle of the functioning of Totality.

A DUET OF ONE p. 75

Noumenon and phenomena, the unmanifest and the manifested, are what might be called the original interrelated or polaric opposites – the one conceives the total potential and the other the totality of what is manifested and sensorially perceptible.

EXPLORATIONS INTO THE ETERNAL p. 26

'I' am the eternal present moment, the 'me' is the conceptual flow of time from the future to the past, a flow that makes the relative present impossible to exist. By the time an event is perceived, cognized and interpreted in consciousness by the mind in duality – the split-mind

– the event has already become the past. The duration of the process of perceiving, cognizing and interpreting an event makes it impossible for an event to exist in the present vis-à-vis the past and the future.

EXPLORATIONS INTO THE ETERNAL p. 79

OPPOSITES

It is necessary to understand the concept of opposites clearly. Everything in life comes in opposites, and everything one values and chooses is one of a pair of opposites. All dimensions are opposites: inside and outside, up and down, high and low, left and right. Our social and aesthetic values are also in terms of opposites: strong and weak, success and failure, beautiful and ugly. Our sciences and philosophies are also in terms of opposites: ontology is concerned with being and non-being, logic with true and false, and epistemology with reality and appearance. Life and living seems to consist of nothing but opposites.

It is the human mind-intellect which refuses to accept the natural interconnectedness of opposites as a fact of life. Life and death become life versus death. Good and evil become good versus evil. Then living becomes one continuous process of choice, and the pursuit of that choice. Intellect does not realize that the separation of opposites is unnatural and means conflict and unhappiness. In not accepting the interrelationship between opposites, it has torn them apart, and human misery is based on this very separation.

Until comparatively recently, that is to say, until Newtonian physics (which prevailed for several centuries) was overthrown by modern physics, the idea of the inner unity of opposites was confined only to mystics, mostly Eastern. But now even science has accepted reality as a union of opposites. Thus, for instance, rest and motion are no longer opposites. According to the relativity theory, 'each is both'. An object for one observer may be at rest whilst for another observer, at the same time, it may be in motion. Similarly, the separation between wave and particle has had to disappear when it was found that in certain circumstances a wave would behave like a particle, and vice versa – so now we have 'wavicles'. There is now no separation of mass from energy, and the old 'opposites' are now seen as two aspects of one reality. This discovery was experienced horrendously by the people of Hiroshima and Nagasaki.

Having said all this about the interrelationship of opposites, the real point will be missed altogether if it is not realized that opposites do not really exist except as a concept. And this is what the sage wants to convey to the disciple. Man's unhappiness rests on the fact that he tries to eradicate one of the opposites – the ugliness, the evil, the weakness, the stupidity. In such attempts, the fact that opposites do not exist at all, other than as a concept, is forgotten. The opposites are an illusion created by the mind-intellect through conceptual separation.

A Duet of One pp. 120–3

When Genesis refers to the fall from grace of Adam and Eve because they gained the 'knowledge of good and evil', the meaning clearly is that their fall was due to a discrimination between 'good and bad', 'useful and useless', 'acceptable and unacceptable', due to a concern about what is of advantage and what is not in the prevailing environment. In other words, man brings in unhappiness for himself when he shows an obsessive preoccupation with security and survival. On the other hand, an understanding acceptance of the polaric duality, on which life and nature are based, would mean a oneness with the universe that enables one to live out one's life with a serenity that would increase the chances of security and survival for the very reason that there is no anxiety that could hamper and curb the free movements in whatever one would normally be doing.

In dualism, the opposites, like the positive and negative, life and death, light and darkness, good and evil, are at war with each other. As far as metaphysical duality is concerned, this is as unthinkable as an electric current without both positive and negative poles. Dualism means pursuing happiness to the exclusion of all unhappiness, pursuing triumph to the exclusion of all defeat, pursuing what is good to the banishment of all that is considered evil – in short, health, wealth and happiness to the absolute exclusion of sickness, poverty and pain. The principle of polaric duality, on the other hand, means the willing *acceptance* of the interrelated opposites as the very basis of both the universe and life therein. Life then becomes an art, holding the two interrelated opposites in balance. As Lao-Tzu puts it, 'knowing the male and keeping the female, one becomes a universal stream; becoming a universal stream, one is not separated from eternal virtue'. Male and female, of course, refers not so much to sex as to the dominant characteristics in the masculine and the feminine. The interrelated opposites, in other words, are like the opposite but insep- arable sides of a coin, the poles of a magnet, or the pulse and interval in any vibration.

EXPLORATIONS INTO THE ETERNAL pp. 28 & 27

PAIN

ut the crux of the problem of experiencing alternating pleasure and pain is not really in the actual experiencing but in aligning it with a misconceived idea of 'time'. While the animal is happy enough with momentary pleasure, man needs enjoyable memories and happy expectations in order to enjoy even his immediate pleasure. Indeed, the memories and expectations are far more real and intense than the present pleasure or pain, because the *habit of looking ahead or behind reduces the present pleasure and increases the present pain*. This habit gives a presence to the dead past and the uncertain future, and an absence to the here and now. The only way to break this habit is to be truly convinced that change – almost continuous and ceaseless change – is the very warp and woof of the manifestation and its functioning that we call 'life'.

Pain is identified as pain only because there is a memory of pleasure. Pain gets intensified by the memory of earlier pleasure. In actual fact, the brain can record only one experience at any one moment. Instead of being fully and alertly aware of a present unpleasant experience, one tries to tackle it in terms of the dead past. In an attempt to avoid the experience one tries to adapt oneself to the unknown present by comparing it with the memory of the past. This might perhaps work in cases where you can get away. An aspirin may relieve a headache. But what about things you cannot escape, like fear? The answer is *to be aware of the fear*. To be intensely aware of the fear is to realize that you *are* the fear, and therefore escape is impossible. Indeed, if naming, defining, and comparing is avoided, every experience becomes a new experience. Then there is no conflict between the experiencer and the experience because there is no resistance.

It has been the experience of most people that when resistance and tension cease, pain becomes manageable. It is no longer a frightening experience. The pain sometimes disappears altogether. When there is no resistance to (and separation from) the pain, there is no longer a problem. Then the desire to escape merges into the pain.

The key to bearing pain is in the unequivocal acceptance of it as the fresh experience of the moment in total relaxation. When this is clearly understood, the question of how to do it should not arise. How to relax? How to accept whatever experience the present moment brings with total receptivity? How to breathe? How to digest the food? To expect answers to such questions is to miss the point altogether. Indeed, that such questions should arise is the clear proof that man has allowed his 'brain' to develop logic and reason – linear thinking – without maintaining a balance with its inherent intuitive wisdom. The result is dissatisfaction, conflict, separation within separation, and a ceaseless vicious circle.

THE FINAL TRUTH p. 223

Even in the case of physical illness, knowing the cause of the illness is half the solution. In the case of psychological illness – unhappiness – knowing the cause really needs no other positive action, because psychological illness has no concrete basis. It is a curious fact that a human being goes to a guru and seeks some positive solution, like a mediation of some kind, to get rid of the psychological illness of unhappiness. The joke is that the psychological illness is the result of seeking something acceptable and now there is a further seeking being done to remove the result of the first seeking! Along with the seeking for happiness comes the further seeking for a spiritual goal called enlightenment. The seeking continues endlessly until frustration results. It is for this reason that the sage comes out with the straight-forward statement that the root cause of the misery in *samsara* (life and living in the world) is 'desire' and desire leads to seeking what is at the moment considered acceptable. In other words, the sage says, 'Give up wanting what is considered acceptable. Be satisfied with What-Is.'

A DUET OF ONE p. 125

Pain as an experience relates only to the object and it is consciousness, as sentience, which makes experiencing possible. Reducing pain
means sentience being held in abeyance, by whatever available means
– deep sleep, sedatives, or hatha-yoga – but the fact remains that it is
the object, the psychosomatic apparatus, that suffers the experience
known as pain. When pain reaches a certain point of tolerance, the
apparatus must express the pain, but this limit of tolerance would
vary from object to object. Where there is understanding, there would
be no identification either with the pain itself or the visible expression
of it. It is not that the sage is immune to pain, but it is possible that
the limit of tolerance would be extended to a certain extent because
of the disidentification. But beyond that point the body would
certainly suffer the pain and express it vocally. The point however, is
that the sage would not be identified with the body, and therefore,
even if the body cried out in pain, such expression of the pain would
be witnessed just like that of any other body. The tolerance of pain
would depend more on the natural constitution of the body than on
the understanding of one's true nature, and would therefore not be an
indication of the 'level' of enlightenment!

Consciousness to Consciousness p. 96

You must always go to the root of the problem. When did the
experience of suffering first start? Do you have any memory of any
suffering, say, a hundred years ago? When did the experience start?
Think about it deeply so that the answers to these questions would
arise within yourself without any words. Is life – living itself – other
than experiencing; experiencing in duration, moment to moment
stretched horizontally? And what is experiencing? Is it not reacting to
an outside stimulus which is interpreted through the senses as an
experience – pleasant and acceptable, or unpleasant and not
acceptable. One does not experience suffering – one suffers an
experience, pleasant or unpleasant.

Now, the basic question you should be concerned with is: *Who (or,
more appropriately, what) is it that suffers an experience?* Let me tell you
straight away: *'I' do not (cannot) suffer any experience, pleasant or*

unpleasant; it is only a 'you' or a 'me' who suffers an experience. This is a very important pronouncement and you should ponder over it deeply.

POINTERS FROM NISARGADATTA MAHARAJ p. 155

PROGRESS

The problem apparently is about 'progress'. Now, who is to make the progress, and progress towards what? I have said this repeatedly and untiringly that *you are the Conscious Presence*, the animating consciousness which gives sentience to phenomenal objects; that *you are not a phenomenal object*, which is merely an appearance in consciousness of those who perceive it. How can an 'appearance' make any 'progress' toward any objective? Now, instead of letting this basic apperception impregnate your very being, what you do is to accept it merely as an ideological thesis and ask the question. How can a conceptual appearance know whether it is making any conceptual progress towards its conceptual liberation?

Perhaps, one wonders, could it be that the surest sign of 'progress' – if one cannot give up the concept – is a total lack of concern about 'progress' and an utter absence of anxiety about anything like 'liberation', a sort of 'hollowness' in one's being, a kind of looseness, an unvolitional surrender to whatever might happen?

POINTERS FROM NISARGADATTA MAHARAJ pp. 153–4

PUPPETRY

The show must go on, the script has been finalized; no actor can change his role according to his preferences – all that he can seemingly do is to play the assigned role to the best of his ability. Indeed, more accurately, even the extent to which he will do his best is part of the total show! Can the puppet decide whether or not it will do its best?!

THE ULTIMATE UNDERSTANDING p. 24

Only a little thought and an honest analysis of the events in one's own life will clearly show that as an apparent entity man does not live his life but that he is *being lived* like a puppet. The attempt by a lived puppet to live what he mistakenly considers his own life is not essentially different from the attempt by a dreamed puppet to live his own life in a dream. The pertinent point is that for both (the lived puppet and the dreamed puppet) the attempts are the only 'reality' they could possibly know, whereas in fact both are puppets and their attempts to live their lives are nothing more than reactions to impulses engendered by psycho-physical conditions over which they have no control. Such conditions may be either inherent to the psychosomatic apparatus or environmental or social or habitual, but the fact remains that the reactions to these conditions are what are considered 'living one's life'. The basic fact is that both the lived puppet and the dreamed puppet are essentially their sentience – and not the physical form – and the sentience of both is nothing but a reflex of the mind, a movement in Consciousness which is all that they are.

THE FINAL TRUTH p. 167

RAMANA MAHARSHI

Ramana Maharshi was the great Jnani Sage of Arunachala who lived all of his adult life in Tiruvannamalai in Tamil Nadu. Ramesh said in Satsang, 'To me, in phenomenality, there is nothing higher than Ramana Maharshi.'

QUOTED BY BLAYNE BARDO IN THE GLOSSARY TO
YOUR HEAD IN THE TIGER'S MOUTH p. 415

Ramana Maharshi says: 'Be without leaving yourself.'
   In other words, go through life without ever forgetting that it is the Source or Primal Energy that is functioning through the programmed psychosomatic apparatus.

Ramana Maharshi accepted that while 'mind' must ultimately be destroyed, it is this very mind which must be used as a stick to aid us to reach a point where the stick can be abandoned.

THE ULTIMATE UNDERSTANDING pp. 190 & 52

Ramana Maharshi said, 'There are only two things: sleep and creation. There is nothing if you go to sleep; you wake up and there is everything. If you learn to "sleep" when awake, you can be just a witness. This is the real truth.'

THE BHAGAVAD GITA p. 32

As Ramana Maharshi often said, the guru's words are to be used like a thorn to remove the thorn of concepts embedded in the heart, and thereafter both the thorns are to be thrown away. That is why in every verse thereafter, he keeps repeating that once the embedded thorn of concepts was removed, he was abiding in the Self and was no longer

129

concerned with any concept of the interrelated opposites. He has seen phenomenality as nothing but a great dream in which the individual is merely a character without any substantial existence.

The Maharshi further explained that actually there is only one state, that of Consciousness or awareness or existence. The three states of waking, dream and deep sleep are transient, but the real state continues to exist all the time. What is present throughout is the impersonal sense of presence. What is absent in the deep sleep state is the personal sense of presence.

In the words of Ramana Maharshi, 'solitude is in the mind'. One might be in the thick of the world and maintain serenity of mind. Such a one is in solitude. Another may stay in a forest, but still be unable to control his mind. Such a man cannot be said to be in solitude. Solitude is a function of the mind. A man attached to desires cannot get solitude wherever he may be, whereas a detached man is always in solitude wherever he may be. Work performed with attachment is a shackle, whereas work performed with detachment does not affect the (apparent) doer. 'One who works like this is, even while working, in solitude.' Solitude means tranquility, serenity, being at peace, unruffled.

As Ramana Maharshi said:
> 'Do not meditate – Be!
> Do not think that you are – Be!
> Do not think about being – you Are!'

The Maharshi was quite clear that in the beginning, when the urge had just turned the mind inward, regular times of formal practice and discipline were good. But he did not recommend long periods of sitting in meditation. As the understanding begins to dawn, if the practices and disciplines are not persisted with stubbornly, a sense of deeper beatitude will arise spontaneously without the intrusion of the 'me'-concept. While one's hands are busy at work, one's head will be cool in silence and solitude. The Maharshi invariably showed his disapproval whenever any of the devotees showed an inclination, or asked for permission to give up their usual mundane activities in order to take up a meditative life.

Ramana Maharshi was equally emphatic against any practices to control the mind. He would say, 'Show me the mind and I shall tell you what to do with it.'* He would assert that the mind, being merely a collection of thoughts, cannot be extinguished by another thought, desire or decision. The mind (the ego, the 'me'-concept) is only fattened by such new thoughts. As Ashtavakra says, the ignorant people (*moodha*) by their seeking only feed the illusion of *samsara*.

Ramana Maharshi, the great master-idler, was once asked by a visitor why he, the Maharshi, did not do some social service or at least go out and preach his own teaching, instead of merely lying about on his couch. The Maharshi calmly asked him, 'How do you know that all that is necessary is not already happening just through my being here?'

You become a master-idler when all sense of personal doership is totally lost. Give up action, give up doing, and you become an idler. Give up the sense of personal doership and let action happen, and you become the master-idler.

A DUET OF ONE pp. 220, 206, 185, 119–20 & 168–9

Ramana Maharshi has described Self-enquiry as the direct method of 'diving into the Heart', seeking the source of the 'me'. He has made it clear that the meditation 'I am not this, I am that', while being useful, is not itself the means of finding that source.

The final truth, as Ramana Maharshi and Nisargadatta Maharaj and all the sages before them have clearly stated, is that there is neither creation nor destruction, neither birth nor death, neither destiny nor free will, neither any path nor any achievement.

THE FINAL TRUTH pp. 189 & 9

* He used the analogy that the mind (ego) dresses itself up as a policeman in order to catch the thief. [Ed.]

As Ramana Maharshi said, 'realization' or 'liberation' is nothing other than 'ridding yourself of the illusion that you are not free'. The same thought was expressed by an ancient Chinese sage as 'never having been bound, you have no need to seek deliverance.'

EXPERIENCING THE TEACHING p. 40

The Maharshi therefore recommended what he called 'self-enquiry' – the constant and *intensely active* enquiry 'who am I?' Such an enquiry stills the mind because the 'me-thought', which is the basis of all conceptualization, suspends all other thoughts and in the process finally itself gets destroyed 'just as the stick used for stirring the burning funeral pyre finally itself gets consumed'.

The great sage of this century, Ramana Maharshi, declared boldly that 'Thinking (conceptualizing) is not man's real nature.' Maharaj was wholly in accord with this statement.

Ramana Maharshi did speak of rebirth, but almost in the same breath he also said that 'life' is nothing but a series of moving pictures on the screen of consciousness. The reference to rebirth was the only base on which conversation with a thoroughly identified individual could go on, and so it was not dropped altogether; otherwise it would have meant a sort of intellectual blackmail; either you accept that the individual is merely a picture on the screen or we do not talk further! Both Ramana Maharshi and Nisargadatta Maharaj had far too much compassion to adopt this attitude, and therefore they talked on a level on which the average person could hope to understand; but at every possible opportunity they would reiterate the final truth that nothing has really happened, that there is no creation and no destruction.

Closely allied to this matter of the image which people form in their minds about the *Jnani* is the question whether there are different levels for the *Jnanis*. This question is dealt with at some length in *Tripura Rahasya*, an ancient work in Sanskrit, which was considered by Ramana Maharshi to be one of the great works on Advaita philosophy.

EXPLORATIONS INTO THE ETERNAL pp. 89, 87, 66 & 59

It was said of Ramana Maharshi that when people chanted hymns in praise of Ramana, he himself would join them in the singing and keep time by clapping his hands like all the others. He had utterly disidentified himself with any entity and was, therefore, totally oblivious to any implications of his actions. The hymns referred to 'Ramana', not to an individual. The *Jnani* really has no individual entity to be embarrassed about, and his psychosomatic apparatus, the body, carries out its normal functions in the normal way without his being aware of them.

POINTERS FROM NISARGADATTA MAHARAJ p. 131

REBIRTH

The future body's personality will be drawn from the totality of the universal consciousness which is the collection of all the 'clouds of images' that keep on getting generated. This total collection gets distributed among new bodies as they are being created, with certain given characteristics which will produce precisely those actions which are necessary to the script of the divine playwright. No individual is concerned as an individual with any previous entity.

CONSCIOUSNESS WRITES p. 85

In this temporal dream play where sentient beings are created and destroyed in thousands every minute, evolution must obviously form the basis of the play of *Nisarga* (Life). In the physicist's bubble chambers, infinitesimally small high-energy 'elementary' particles (many of which have a lifetime much shorter than a millionth of a second) collide and annihilate each other or create new particles that give rise to a fresh chain of events in manifestation. Similarly, every baby born would be expected to play a particular role in the dream play so that the play may proceed on its inevitable course. The sentient being, which as a mere appearance in consciousness cannot possibly have independent choice of action, is created in order to fulfill a particular function (whether as a Hitler or a Gandhi or an insignificant individual) and not the other way around. It is not that a new function is created just so that the individual soul or animus (or whatever) be punished or rewarded for his karma in a previous birth! The supposed individual in any case is not an independent, autonomous entity – he merely carries out his *destined* function which paves the way for the destined function of another supposed individual in the temporal future, according to the scenario of the dream play. There would necessarily be continuity between the form that dies and the new form that is born because evolution must go on, and nature does not start from scratch each time. This is no doubt the reason why Mozart could compose music when he was twelve and Jnaneshwar could produce the *Jnaneshwari* at the age of sixteen. But there is no reason for a conceptual individual to identify himself with a series of births in the temporal manifestation.

The Buddha has said, 'As there is no self, there is no transmigration of self; but there are deeds and continued effects of deeds. These deeds are being done but there is no doer. There is no entity that migrates, no self is transferred from one place to another; but there is a voice uttered here and the echo comes back.' Could it have been said any better or any clearer?

EXPERIENCING THE TEACHING p. 51

Let us come back to your problem of rebirth. What is 'born', the objective body, will, in due course, 'die'; thereafter it will be dissolved i.e. irrevocably annihilated, the life-force will leave the body and mingle with the air outside. The objective part of what was once a sentient being will be destroyed, never to be reborn as the same body. And consciousness is not an object, not a 'thing' at all – therefore, *consciousness, as something non-objective, cannot be 'born', cannot 'die' and certainly cannot be 'reborn'.*

These are indisputable facts, are they not – facts about the phenomenally manifested sentient being? As a process of the functioning of the noumenon, manifestation of phenomena takes place, in which forms get created and forms get destroyed. Who is born? And who dies? And who is to be reborn?

If this is so, you may ask how does the concept of karma, causality and rebirth arise at all? The answer is that instead of a phenomenon being accepted as a manifestation of the unmanifest (and thus an aspect of the non-phenomenal noumenon), a mistaken identification with a pseudo-entity takes place and a phantom with a supposed autonomous existence gets created. This phantom is supposed to have choice of decision and action. It is this phantom that is supposed to be born, to live, to suffer and to die. And in this process, it is this phantom who becomes liable to the process of causality known as karma, accepts the supposed 'bondage' and 'rebirth', and seeks an imagined 'liberation'.

In other words, over the natural process of the manifestation of phenomena gets superimposed a phantom-self with a supposed autonomous, independent existence, and on this phantom-self is loaded the concept of the resultant effects of the imagined volitional actions – i.e. karma, bondage and rebirth!

How did the idea of rebirth arise at all? It was perhaps conceived as some sort of an acceptable working theory to satisfy the simpler people who were not intelligent enough to think beyond the parameters of the manifested world.

POINTERS FROM NISARGADATTA MAHARAJ
pp. 124–5 & 184

SCIENCE

Perhaps the most significant conclusion arrived at by the physicist in recent times is the statement that no object exists unless it is observed. The observation can only happen through an object which does not exist unless it is observed. And an object is a three-dimensional thing extended in space and observable through the serialized duration called time. And, 'space-time' is not an object! Therefore, the only conclusion is that an object does not exist – that the 'observed' object is an illusion, and the observing can only be a noumenal functioning.

Sir Isaac Newton's physics assumed that the future of the world was precisely predictable from the state of the present. However, the new physics of quantum mechanics has come to the confident conclusion that the future is *not* determined totally by the past. In other words, quantum mechanics says that the Source, or Consciousness, has a causal influence on the future. At any point in time, we are told, out of the thousands of probabilities, one probability collapses into an actuality in the present moment. This scientific conclusion is precisely what the sages have been saying for ages.

In the functioning of the universe, the dualistic analysis of the physicists resembles that of the sages to an astonishing degree. But the fact of the matter is that it must necessarily be so, because the descriptions of the sages – like those of the scientists – being 'descriptions' must necessarily be dualistic. What the sages describe is what they see objectively – mountains and rivers are still mountains and rivers – but the important distinction is that, at the same time, they are fully aware that what they see, subjectively, is the Source from which the mountains and rivers have appeared. And, most important, when the seeing ceases, they are what has been described in the Hindu scriptures as *Sat-Chit-Ananda*.

In other words, what the sages apperceive – intuitively know – is that there is no subject *see*-ing an object but only a seeing, 'pure perception': think*ing* but no thinker, do*ing* but no doer, experienc*ing* but no experiencer.

THE ULTIMATE UNDERSTANDING pp. 135 & 128–9

Every human organism is conceived and created with certain given characteristics: physical, mental, intellectual, temperamental. No person has any choice or control concerning his parents and, therefore, in what environmental conditions he would be born. In other words, no person has any choice over his genes – DNA; nor does he have any choice over the conditioning he would get in the environment in which he is born. Therefore, it is a fact that he has no choice over either his genes or his environmental conditioning. And the DNA plus the conditioning is the basic cause of a person's personality, his psyche, based on his natural characteristics as developed by the environmental conditioning. His 'faith', his outlook on life and living, will therefore also be based on these factors.

THE BHAGAVAD GITA p. 106

Now, science has come to the aid of the mystic. The sub-atomic physicist has come to this conclusion, after probing the behaviour of sub-atomic particles, known as quantum mechanics which puts the matter of causation completely in the background. The quantum theory of Planck – the new 'law' of Indeterminacy – replaces causality, and is now more or less accepted where the microcosmos is concerned, and it seems that there is really no reason why it should not apply to the macrocosmos because size must be taken to be as relative as anything else.

Until the quantum theory came along, certain 'realistic' assumptions were taken for granted by all scientists, and it is these arbitrary assumptions which created an almost insurmountable barrier to the understanding of what the mystic knew intuitively. These assumptions were:

   a) there is a 'real' world whose existence is independent of any
      observer;

b) in this 'real' world, any phenomenon that is sensorially perceptible must have a physical cause, and therefore valid conclusions could be drawn about cause and effect from consistent observations;

c) physically separate objects and well-separated events must be regarded as truly distinct. Thus if a shell is exploded and certain fragments spin off and have parted company, they cannot thereafter influence one another.

The quantum theory, whilst passing the supreme test of any scientific theory that it 'worked', had three very peculiar features which irked and irritated many scientists of the day. They were:

a) the theory does not predict unique outcomes but only states *probabilities*;

b) to add insult to injury, as it were, it accepts 'uncertainty not merely as an irritating headache but as something one must live with; the uncertainty is accepted as an intrinsic feature of the sub-atomic world';

c) it comes to the fantastic conclusion that the observer and the object he observes cannot always be considered as separate and distinct (which is what the mystic has always been saying).

Even Einstein, whose 'equations of relativity' were the basis of the quantum mechanics, could not wholeheartedly accept the principle of uncertainty and the transcending of objective reality. As Descartes had earlier exclaimed that 'God cannot deceive us', Einstein repeatedly asserted that he just could not accept that 'God plays dice with the universe'. Both laboured under metaphysical dogmas and could not grasp the idea of the divine spirit as being at once transcendental to and immanent in the manifested universe. Werner Heisenberg, on the other hand, averred that the quantum theory excludes a totally objective description of nature based on the premise of a physical world existing independently of the human observer.

The new vision of the universe thus gives up the long prevailing view of it from a materialistic viewpoint, and now seems to approximate the Eastern vision of not physical reality but a metaphysical reality. The new formulations of physics in ordinary language, devoid of the mathematical jargon, are 'translogical' and therefore seem more like the paradoxical aphorisms of the Upanishads or the riddle-like koans of Zen Buddhism. For instance, Sir James Jeans describes the phenomenal universe as a cosmic sphere the inside of which would seem to be made of 'empty space welded to empty time'.

This idea of the 'holarchy' or hierarchy has been stressed merely to point out that no individual – as observer or otherwise – can remain outside the universe as a separate point of observation or action with total autonomy. His existence, such as it is, can be only in relevance to the entire universe and all the interrelated phenomena therein. Moreover, the orderliness in which the universe operates is quite beyond the capacity of the intellect to understand, and this now seems to be appreciated by the modern physicist with the virtual disappearance of the sharp separation between subject and object, observer and observed; and the observer, like the mystic, is now accepted as an active 'participant' in the *experience* (rather than an experiment), forming one whole with whatever is being observed. In other words, all there is, is the *experience*, without the necessity of any material substratum as the object of which the event is an experience. What this means, therefore, is that nature itself exhibits a holistic tendency to form wholes that are greater than the sum of its parts inasmuch as, in the physicist's terms, the proton and the electron do not pre-exist within the neutron but *something new is created*. If the universe is imagined as a vast quantum object, it divides itself into the multitude of living beings, planets and stars only if it is viewed in the divisive objectifying perspective, and not otherwise. Any divisive separation is only notional.

This is a startling conclusion at which the modern physicist has arrived, and the layman today could well wonder if he is listening to a Western modern physicist or to an Eastern mystic. But the physicist has not arrived at the ultimate conclusion because he has to labour under the limitations of the intellect. Mind obviously cannot find its own source. On the contrary, it is only when the mind is at the end of its tether and gives up the struggle and becomes a void – the void of fullness – that the physicist will KNOW the whole mystery and get all the answers. However, the joke of it all is that *then* – in that state – the physicist will no longer remain the physicist wanting to know the answer to questions, but will have merged and become the absolute subject, beyond all experience, beyond all questions and answers.

The modern scientist, through his imaginative researches based on a thoroughly open mind, prepared to accept and consider anything that the researchers might reveal – however unbelievable or incredible – seems to be arriving at a frame of mind whereby the phenomenal universe becomes more and more intelligible only through the questioning of the very concepts, notions and scientific beliefs which were earlier most taken for granted. The modern scientist seems to be arriving at the conclusion which the mystic had arrived at many centuries ago, that the phenomenal manifestation is a game – *Lila* – of hide-and-seek, that a new discovery would have been much more easily located if the scientists had but known where to seek, and that the best places to hide are those where no one would think of looking! Indeed, the modern scientist seems on the threshold of arriving at, or going back to ('REVERSING' as Nisargadatta Maharaj was fond of saying) the ancient Advaita aphorism: TAT TWAM ASI: That Thou Art. He is about to jump off the highest cliff of scientific intellect into the intuitive void of the mystic to find out for himself whether, as the mystic avers, the seeker and the sought are one, and to experience for himself whether the universe is indeed a dynamic, inseparable whole in which the observer is essentially included.

That the constituents of matter and the basic manifested phenomena involving them are not only interdependent and interconnected, but that it is possible to understand them only as integrated parts of a whole and not in isolation, is the conclusion arrived at by various models of sub-atomic physics in diverse ways. The mystic has always included the human observer and his consciousness (strictly speaking, 'his' consciousness would not be correct because it is universal consciousness which pervades all sentient beings) in the universal interwoveness. The sub-atomic physicist too now finds that he cannot talk about the properties of an object because such properties become meaningful only in the context of an interaction between the object and the observer. Indeed, the new physicist finds that he becomes so involved in the world that is being observed that he actually 'influences' the properties of the objects that are being observed. Many modern physicists consider that this intimate involvement between the observer and the observed thing is perhaps the most important feature of the quantum theory, and have therefore adopted the word 'participator' instead of 'observer'. The mystic has always said that his 'knowledge' is not observation by any means but that it is an intuitive experience which obviously comports the idea of the fullest possible participation to the extent that both the observer and the observed disappear in the noumenal function of observe-ING. As an Upanishad has put it, when everything has become only one's own self, then whom and whereby would one see, or smell, or taste? The modern physicist cannot, of course, experience this unity of all things as does the mystic because he must necessarily at present work in the context of a specified, limited framework. He must content himself with the intellectual conviction which is supported by his sub-atomic models that things and events in the whole world are woven into an inseparable 'net of endless, mutually conditioned relations'.

EXPLORATIONS INTO THE ETERNAL pp. 144–5, 112 & 108

It is really a mystery how a single thought gives rise to a series of events which have a series of repercussions on a number of people. It happens to be a 'mystery', however, because as Niels Bohr said to Albert Einstein, 'God is not really playing dice with the universe but it only seems so to us because we do not have the full information which God has.' Repeatedly, therefore, I find I have to say that all is part of the functioning of Totality, and all 'one' can do is to witness whatever is happening. Actually, when this is truly understood, it is also simultaneously realized that there is no 'one' to witness, that witnessing takes place by itself, and that if there is a feeling of some 'one' witnessing, it will almost certainly mean a personal 'observing' accompanied, however surreptitiously, by comparing and judging, however unconscious.

CONSCIOUSNESS TO CONSCIOUSNESS p. 55

SCRIPTURES

What we regard as scriptures today, were at one time written by some human being, in your terms some enlightened human being, and when he wrote that scripture, or gave his talks, he must obviously have had certain people in mind to whom his words were addressed. It would therefore not be right to accept such words as suitable for all types of people. Then as time passes, there is the inescapable danger of various interpolations being made, and certain inconvenient portions being deleted to suit the changing conditions and circumstances.

EXPERIENCING THE TEACHING p. 35

SEARCH

All search must necessarily end in failure. How can an eye see that which sees? Whatever is conceived as 'that' must necessarily be that-which-is-not, because 'that' is what is conceiving. How can conceiving conceive that which is conceiving? Indeed, what the sage implies here is that in the very realization of this fact what seems like a failure becomes the successful end of the search. What is then realized is that the duality of the sought and the seeker just does not exist. And if it is realized that 'that' which the seeker is seeking is 'this' which is doing the seeking, is it not also significantly realized that if the seeking is unnecessary and futile all methods and practices involved in the seeking must be equally unnecessary and futile? Also, that the integral apperception of this situation must itself be the instant awakening which would in course of time settle down into the undisturbed state of total deliverance?

EXPERIENCE OF IMMORTALITY, p. 222

SEEING

True perceiving means perceiving the illusoriness of the pseudo-subject, the sole factor which prevents our BEING that subjective unicity. The moment this true perceiving, this understanding becomes spontaneous, we would be experiencing the Teaching, because then, in the words of the great Chinese sage Shen-hui, we would be having 'silent identification with non-being'.

EXPERIENCING THE TEACHING p. 77

True seeing – seeing the totality in its inevitable functioning – soon becomes a habit which then transforms itself into true living in which, because of the acceptance of the totality of functioning, living becomes freed of tension, work assumes a beauty of its own by being dissociated from the rewards, action becomes more spontaneous and intuitive, and life in general becomes more natural and altogether more enjoyable. When one sees the enormity of the manifestation as a whole, one cannot but understand the inevitability of its functioning in accordance with an overall plan which could not possibly fit in with the limited parameters of an individual's intellect.

EXPLORATIONS INTO THE ETERNAL p. 260

SEEKERS

Most 'spiritual seekers' have only a very confused idea about what they are seeking. They may call it 'enlightenment' or 'Self-realization', but they do not really have any clear idea about it. All they feel is that it is not something connected with life in this world, that it is something out of this world, something unknown. But anything unknown, out of this world, can only be the one Supreme Reality – the ONE without a second, and therefore any thing or person who wants this One Reality can only be an illusion. The total apperception of this simple fact is 'enlightenment' or 'Self-realization'.

A seeker seeking salvation through a particular path is in fact trying to get out of a hole he has never been in: the effort itself becomes the hole.

THE ULTIMATE UNDERSTANDING pp. 39 & 19

It is part of the cosmic joke that, even having intellectually understood that objective understanding is by itself not only futile but could actually be a hindrance, you cannot stop seeking such objective understanding. The spontaneous urge which turned you into a seeker in the first place will not let you stop seeking. Yet this is necessary, because it is only the deepest frustration generated by the objective comprehender which will be the catalyst, at the appropriate time (over which you can have no control) for that very objective comprehension to be suddenly transformed into subjective apperception. As Ma Tzu, the Chinese Master put it, 'In the Tao there is nothing to discipline oneself in. If there is any discipline in it, the completion of such discipline means the destruction of the Tao. But if there is no discipline whatever in the Tao, one remains an ignoramus.'

All the causes of confusion and discontentment – desire, greed, envy, pride etc. – are not independent phenomena but merely the manifestations of the identified ego. It is important to understand this. It is only because this is not clearly apprehended in its depth – though it might have been superficially comprehended by the mind – that people visit 'godmen'. They ask those 'godmen' to show them the way to get rid of the confusion and conflict in which they find themselves all the time. In a way this is a real joke inasmuch as they want the identified 'me' to enjoy something which can come about only when the 'me' disappears. It is even more of a joke that such 'seekers' go to such great lengths, not only spending a lot of money on religious rituals, but often going in for quite strenuous physical and mental disciplines and practices. In the end all these efforts result in frustration because the very basis of such practices is the 'me'-concept *wanting something*.

To those seekers who seek enlightenment not out of dispassion towards sense objects but as an object that will yield them pleasure and happiness infinitely greater than what sense objects have so far given them, the transformation enlightenment actually brings about (which they see as a sort of listlessness) seems to them confusing and discouraging. The dispassion which is at the root of a true spiritual seeking is neither the dulling of the senses through an excess of sensual enjoyment nor the suppression of senses through forced disciplines. Both these lead to frustration. It is only after the senses have experienced their respective objects and a sense of dispassion has arisen through a deep conviction that life and living must have a meaning that is deeper than merely enjoying the pleasure of the senses, that the genuine seeking begins.

Where the intellect is immature, and the individual keeps seeking (and wanting) enlightenment as an object for himself or herself, the wanting and the seeking continues to be the bondage. The knowledge that is sought itself becomes the bondage because such knowledge is not true understanding (without any individual comprehender) but an experience enjoyed by the seeker as an individual. Such experiences are often misconceived and misunderstood as enlightenment. It is not realized that it is only the individual object that can experience anything and that therefore, enlightenment cannot happen so long as there exists the individual wanting to experience enlightenment. And it is this kind of spiritual seeking which lands the individual in the confusion of an organized religion. The tenets, the concepts and the dos and don'ts of organized religions are in constant conflict not only with one another within itself (which leads to the necessity of 'interpretation' of the written word) but also with those of other organized religions.

A DUET OF ONE pp. 150 & 181, 103 & 99

While there are few spiritual aspirants at any one time ready to receive the guru's instruction like a spark for gunpowder, there is a very large number of aspirants who are like wet coal and would therefore need considerable preliminary preparation to purify the mind in order to be able to receive *any* spiritual instruction. For this latter type on the lowest level, Nisargadatta Maharaj would recommend listening to spiritual singing (*bhajan*), counting beads and repeating His name, etc. In between these two extreme levels is the class of aspirants who are neither the spiritual gunpowder nor the wet coal. These belong to the dry charcoal category who need a certain amount of discipline, a certain amount of spiritual heat to be prepared before the combustion can take place. It is for this middle class that the practice of Self-enquiry is prescribed. The aim of Self-enquiry is to discover by direct experience – not merely at the intellectual level – that there is no such thing as a mind. The discovery relates to the fact that every conscious activity – whether of the body or of the mind – is inevitably based on the existence of the 'me'-concept. It is further discovered, again by direct experience, that the 'me' is not an independent or autonomous entity but merely a mental modification, an illusory reflection of the Self. Through the continuous and ceaseless use of Self-enquiry (which need not interfere with the work of daily life), the 'me'-concept disappears along with all the conceptualization based on it. And when this unnecessary obstruction is removed, Self-realization happens. In this state of enlightenment there exists no individual thinker, no individual observer, no individual do-er – indeed no 'individual' at all. All there is is the sense of presence *as such* – I Am. The absence of 'me' is the presence of 'I'.

It is of utmost importance to understand the significance of this classification. The very basis of the teaching is that there is no such thing as an independent individual entity and that the supposed individual is merely a concept, a mental modification, an illusion. If this is clearly understood and accepted with deep conviction, it would naturally follow that enlightenment is merely a phenomenon, a happening that occurs as part of the totality of functioning in the universal play.

This most important aspect of the matter is often overlooked by the spiritual teacher who in his very exegesis unfortunately praises the 'one' at the higher level and, directly or indirectly, sneers at the 'one' at the lower level. He compares the aspirant at the top to a racehorse who puts in his best as soon as he sees the whip, whereas the aspirant at the lowest level will not be able to grasp the teaching, even if Shiva became his guru.

THE FINAL TRUTH p. 172

Spiritual seekers are lost children in a conceptual forest created by their own imagination.

THE ULTIMATE UNDERSTANDING p. 8

SELF

True happiness (real quietude) consists not in volitional effort to achieve happiness but only in understanding what Self-abidance is, and Self-abidance is not something to be acquired but something which arises spontaneously when the mind is free of the concepts of right and wrong, the acceptable and the unacceptable, and all such pairs of opposites. The sage tells us that enlightenment or Self-abidance is our natural state. It does not need to be acquired. Any personal, volitional effort means only strengthening the ego, the 'me', which is itself the obstruction which covers and hides our original state. What is more, the sage assures us that the true understanding of this very fact is all that is necessary for the seeker! When the understanding is true and deep, the question 'I have understood what you are saying, but having understood your theory, what do I actually do in everyday life?' does not arise. It cannot arise. If it does arise, the understanding has not been either true or deep enough.

A DUET OF ONE p. 118

When the Self has been attained, nothing has been attained! The inner and the outer, the Self and the non-self are mere words without any significance or substance, used only for the benefit of the ignorant. When the external object is seen as such, the pseudo-subject is created. Actually all there is is the see-*ing*, there is neither the see-*er* nor the object seen. When the mnemonic impressions have ceased, the pseudo-subject no longer exists and without the supposed subject, the object cannot exist either. The noumenon, as the subject, exists because of the object, and the phenomenal object is but a reflection of the subject. Duality can exist only as the interrelated opposite of non-duality. *Where is the question of union or unity if all there is is unicity?* The goldness of the gold is always there. The question of duality arises only when there is a name and form as a bracelet. That which is beyond all interrelated opposites is the Absolute, the Brahman. When there is apperception of this truth, all duality and non-duality disappear. What remains is not expressible in words. Such apperception happens only through Self-enquiry. As long as words are used to denote a truth, duality in the form of the interrelated opposites is inevitable. Though words are necessary to direct the attention of the ignorant to the truth, words are *not* the truth.

The direct experience of the Self is known as *jnana* or Self-realization. There is often an avoidable misunderstanding because the term *jnana* is taken to mean that there is a *separate* individual who has knowledge of the Self. It is astonishing how persistent this misunderstanding remains. Unless care is taken to understand the term *jnana* in its full significance, the spiritual aspirant will base his quest on a totally erroneous belief. The state of Self-awareness cannot come about unless the notion of a separate individual has been totally erased. In the state of Self-awareness there cannot exist any particular individual knower of the Self. *Jnana* is a direct, subjective awareness of the one indivisible reality in which *jnana* is not an object of understanding or experiencing, and in which the subject-object relationship has ceased to exist. In fact, although the term '*jnani*' is used for the purpose of communication, to denote 'one' who is firmly established in the state of Self-awareness, it must be clearly understood that the term '*jnani*' is in reality a misnomer inasmuch as the *jnani* is not to be taken as a separate individual.

THE FINAL TRUTH pp. 232 & 170

151

SELF-ENQUIRY

R amana Maharshi made it perfectly clear that his teaching – 'find out "Who am I?"' – was simply not an intellectual exercise (and yet very many people continue to treat it as such), but a technique for focusing the split-mind of subject-object exclusively on the Subject, that is to say, Consciousness, or the pure, impersonal Subjectivity, so that the basic dualism of subject-object could be dissolved in this focusing. Subject and object are then apperceived as not two: 'I' am both subject and object, alternatively in duality (other observer-subject becomes the object when the object becomes the observer-subject), and fused in Unicity.

THE ULTIMATE UNDERSTANDING p. 157

For the quieting of the mind there is no means more effective than Self-enquiry. The mind may subside by other means, but it will rise again. Self-enquiry is a direct method. Other methods are practiced while retaining the ego, and therefore many doubts arise, leaving the ultimate obstacle still to be dealt with. In Self-enquiry, it is only the final question that is tackled from the very beginning.

Self-enquiry is the direct path to Self-realization. It removes the obfuscation that covers the never-realized Self. Such obfuscation is itself the creation of mind and most other methods retain the mind as the basis of the method. To ask the mind to destroy the mind is like making the thief the policeman, or putting the arsonist in charge of fire engines! The only way to make the mind cease its outward activities is to turn it inward.

By steady and continuous investigation into the nature of the mind, the mind gets transformed into that to which the 'me' owes its existence. The mind must necessarily depend on something gross for its existence. Identification with the body as a separate entity is what 'mind' (ego) is as 'me'. It is only after the 'me' arises that the 'you' and 'he' and the other personal pronouns arise. It is for this reason that the source of the 'me' is to be sought by Self-enquiry.

The mind turned outward results in thoughts and objectivizing. Turned inward, it destroys all other thoughts. Then the 'me' concept finally destroys itself 'like a stick used for stirring a burning funeral pyre itself gets consumed'.

The notion of the existence of the universe can arise only when the spirit of Self-enquiry is absent. 'I' being present before the universe could ever appear, no notion about the universe and anything or anyone therein could possibly concern this 'I' that I am (and each of us truly is). Whatever I may be engaged in doing in this life, I cannot be disturbed by any happening because I am beyond all duality and non-duality, as in deep sleep. It is as if I am in deep sleep although actively engaged in life.

This is what is achieved by Self-enquiry. It is not merely a matter of repeating 'Who am I?' like a mantra, in which case it would not have much value. The aim of Self-enquiry is to focus the mind at its source to the exclusion of all thoughts and concepts. It is not at all a matter of the 'me' searching for the 'I', or the 'I' searching for the 'me'. In one case the thief himself is appointed the policeman and seeks to find the thief, and in the other, the 'I' is not at all concerned with the 'me'. It is not a matter of seeking the source of thoughts based on the 'me' and then wandering into the source of particular thoughts, into the realms of memory and perception. All this mental activity would belong to the 'me' concept, the mind which itself is the thief trying to locate the thief. What is to be enquired into is the source of the 'me' (mind) and not memory or perception which are the attributes of the mind itself. Perception or memory or any other experience, being only a modification of the mind, concerns the very 'me' whose source is to be located through Self-enquiry.

Self-enquiry means enquiry into:
a) the nature of the Self
b) the nature of the world
c) the nature of the Truth.
Enquire into the nature of Truth thus.

Enquiry into the nature of the Self dispels this mistaken identity, and the very dispassion that starts this enquiry is sufficient to bring about the annihilation of that illusory entity, which has no independent nature of its own.

The instruction from the guru needs to be contemplated seriously.

The prescribed method is Self-enquiry, the basis of which is the focusing of attention on the inner feeling of 'I' (not 'me'), the sense of impersonal presence. In the early stages, the practice of Self-enquiry is necessarily an intellectual activity, but soon the intellectual perception of the 'I' gives place to a subjective experience which is totally dis-identified from objects and relative thoughts. The final stage of Self-enquiry is reached when an effortless awareness of I Am prevails, though not incessantly. Self-realization is when this effortless awareness is incessant, but the important point is that this state cannot be 'achieved' for the simple reason that the 'me' who is supposed to make the effort is on his way to annihilation.

The practice of Self-enquiry or awareness or witnessing is a gentle, negative technique − if at all it can be so called − to get rid of the positive conditioning that has accumulated over a long period, and is totally different from the usually oppressive and repressive methods of controlling the mind. Curiously near to it is the method of surrender to God as a means of achieving Self-realization, or more accurately, liberation from bondage. The path of surrender is generally associated with *bhakti* (devotional practice) which is essentially dualistic in nature. The point that is often missed or ignored in such devotional practices is that the 'me' concept (illusory individual entity) gets stronger and stronger. The separation between the individual and his 'God' gets wider and wider, if there is a motive or purpose or a desire to be satisfied, behind the devotional practices. *Even the desire for liberation or enlightenment will make the surrender incomplete* or partial because the supposed individual makes an effort to get or achieve something in return. It is then only a business transaction; there is desire behind the efforts.

The only true surrender is when there is no 'one' to ask questions or to expect anything. This means surrendering the *total* responsibility for one's life, for all one's thoughts and actions, to a higher power, God, or Self. Obviously, such self-surrender presupposes that one cannot have any will or desire of one's own – which means in effect the acceptance of the fact that there is no individual entity with ability to act independently of God. This actually amounts to a constant awareness that it is only the Self that prevails and that the supposed individual is truly an irrelevance in the totality of functioning. In other words, there is really no significant difference between Self-enquiry and surrender because in both, the 'me' is finally to be isolated and annihilated.

THE FINAL TRUTH pp. 177–209

Self-enquiry is essentially an enquiry into the nature of man because, whatever man may think of the world outside, whatever man may conceive of God as the creator, all of it would be conjecture and conceptualization. The only thing of which man can be certain, the only thing he KNOWS is that he exists, that he is alive. In deep sleep, he is quite unaware of the world outside or of the creator of that world, and yet when he wakes up he again KNOWS not only that he is alive but that he was alive even during the period of his sleep. This is the basis of the Nisargadatta teachings.

It is the Guru who guides the disciple in the latter's enquiry into the nature of the self. This knowledge of the Self is beyond that knowledge which is the polaric counterpart of ignorance; it is the kind of knowledge which has existed from time immemorial, indeed since before time ever was; in fact that knowledge is itself BEINGNESS-HERE-AND-NOW.

EXPLORATIONS INTO THE ETERNAL p. 39

After pursuing my enquiry to its logical conclusion what have I arrived at? The whole thing is really simple, if only one sees the picture clearly. What is this 'me' that I am concerned with? The immediate answer, of course, is – 'this me, this body'. But then the body is only a psychosomatic apparatus. What is the most important element in this apparatus which qualifies it to be known as a sentient being? It is undoubtedly the consciousness without which this apparatus, while perhaps technically alive, would be useless as far as its functioning is concerned. This consciousness obviously needs a physical construct in which to manifest itself. So, consciousness depends upon the body. But what is the body made of? How does the body come into existence? The body is merely a growth in the woman's womb during a period of about nine months, the growth of what is conceived by the union of the male and female sexual fluids. These fluids are the essence of the food consumed by the parents. Basically, therefore, both consciousness and the body are made of, and are sustained by, food. Indeed, the body itself is food – one body being the food of some other body. When the food-essence, the vital sexual fluids, grows from conception into a tiny body and is delivered out of the mother's womb, it is called 'birth'. And when this food essence gets decayed due to age or illness and the psychosomatic apparatus happens to get destroyed, it is called 'death'. This is what happens all the time – the objective universe projecting and dissolving innumerable forms; the picture keeps on changing all the time. But how am 'I' concerned with this? I am merely the witness to all this happening. Whatever happens during the period of the happening, in each case, affects only the psychosomatic apparatus, not the 'I' that I am.

EXPLORATIONS INTO THE ETERNAL p. 47

Self-enquiry must necessarily begin with the 'me'. It is only in those extraordinarily few cases where there is instant acceptance of the guru's pronouncement that the 'me' is an illusory concept (and that all the body-mind organisms are merely the instruments through which the Totality or Consciousness are the only subjective do-er functions) that there is no need for the process of Self-enquiry.

Self-enquiry must necessarily begin with the 'me' and the mind-intellect. But in such an enquiry the intellect unwittingly lays a trap, conceals it with a lot of concepts, builds an elephant pit, and then falls into it itself! It is for this reason that Ramana Maharshi says – or implies – that intellect can only ask the question 'Who (or what) am I?' Intellect, it must be at once understood, cannot provide the answer because it *does not know – it cannot know*: such knowledge cannot be

156

objective, but only a subjective experience of I Am. You cannot *know* deep sleep, you can only talk about it in the waking state!

Therefore, to ask questions such as 'Who (or what) is It that lives my life?', and 'What is my relationship with It?', is to lay a trap of conceptualization into which the mind-intellect falls very quickly and reaches the depths of despair and desperation. And then arise all sorts of doubts and problems which thrive on the 'experiences' which personal efforts and *sadhana* sometimes bring about. Thus, one 'sees a light' or 'hears a sound' while sitting in meditation! But the point is that whenever any light is seen or sound is heard or an experience is felt, there has to be some 'one' who sees or hears or feels. The question therefore must arise: 'Who (or what) is this someone?' And the mind-intellect is back into the elephant pit.

The quantum jump out of this conceptual elephant pit cannot come out of any phenomenal effort which itself has brought about this situation. It can only happen when the self-generated impersonal functioning of Totality is suddenly realized, in which realization the 'me', the 'someone,' gets annihilated. And the joke – or the tragedy – is that such realization can only *happen* at the appropriate time which is quite beyond the control of the phenomenal seeker in the form of a body-mind mechanism. This realization is the sudden end result of the conviction, the constantly (mentally) repeated irresistible refrain 'it does not matter – nothing matters'. Matter to whom? To the 'me', of course, because the 'me' is in the process of being annihilated, and even this annihilation does not matter!

CONSCIOUSNESS TO CONSCIOUSNESS p. 70

Similarly, Self-enquiry differs fundamentally from any kind of psychiatric treatment because the latter merely aims at producing a normal integrated individual ego whereas Self-enquiry aims at *transcending* the bounds of the human individual. The common ground is that both bring up hidden thoughts and impurities buried in the depths of the mind. The point is that these *thoughts spring up spontaneously, and when thus exposed, through Self-enquiry, are promptly extinguished.*

THE FINAL TRUTH p. 192

SELF-REALIZATION

Having gone through six chapters of the book, the reader would perhaps be justified in wondering where he is being led. Indeed, it is only the self-realized person (in fact there is no such thing as a 'self-realized person') who would at once *know* and appreciate the subtlety with which the sage is leading the devotee-reader towards the realization of his real nature. The average reader, however, could be excused if he had the feeling that he was being 'taken for a ride'. Indeed he *is* being taken for a ride around the world and brought back to the starting point and thus made to understand that he (not as the individual 'me', the separate entity that he thinks he is, but as the subjective 'I') cannot be 'taken' anywhere, by anyone, at any time, for the reason that he – as 'I' – is himself spaceless and timeless; and that, as 'I', he is himself infinity and intemporality, and it is only within space and time, that there can be any manifestation or movement.

EXPERIENCE OF IMMORTALITY, p. 126

SEX

About the question that you ask: sexual distraction – who is distracted?! Remember Yang-Chu: 'Let the ear hear what it longs to hear, the eye see what it longs to see, the nose smell what it longs to smell, the mouth speak what it wants to speak, let the body have every comfort that it craves, let the mind do as it will.' Why associate your self, why identify with the body at all? Sometimes it may be that you are less hungry than at other times. Why think in terms of 'you' being less hungry or more hungry – why not there is less hunger or more hunger! Then, when there is disassociation or dis-identification with whatever happens to the body-mind mechanism – including a greater or a lesser tendency towards sex – the prevailing tendencies of the body-mind are merely witnessed *without any comparing or judging*. In such witnessing, the fact that certain changes are taking place is witnessed, without even relating such changes to 'my' body. This is the point: to whichever body such changes may relate, the basic point is that it is the body to which the changes relate.

CONSCIOUSNESS WRITES p. 20

SOURCE

When one refers to the Source, by whatever name, one is likely to miss the significance of what is said: there is a 'self' (which is not) seeking for its 'real nature', that is the Source or Being. What is truly to be realized is that one has to be rid of the idea of both the self and the Being.

The point is that the Source, the Void, that is the complete PLENITUDE, is not Being but Non-being. In other words, what is intensely required to be apperceived is the ubiquitous pre-existence of Nothing – the Energy that is only potential – out of which some thing can appear: out of the potential, the actualization; out of Non-manifestation, manifestation.

The pure Subject, the Source, without the slightest touch of objectivity, can never die because it contains nothing that can come into existence or be extinguished. Only objects that are created can be born and can die. The pure Subject, the Source, can only be Eternity – *Aeternitas* – beyond the concept of time. Perhaps it was this very intuitive understanding which enabled a child of five, at the end of a dissertation by the father on 'life and death', to say with utter confidence, 'I am never going to die.'

By the Grace of the Source, in due course, comes the astonishing Awakening that life is nothing but a living dream. And then one is engulfed in an obliterating embrace of Unicity, in which what-is-in-the-moment is unconditionally accepted.

It is, therefore, only dis-identification with a supposed entity which will suspend the exercising of the conceptual volition and the conceptualizing, the cause of the conceptual bondage. What would remain then is only an identification, without volition, for the body-mind organism to function according to the Will of the Source (or according to the Cosmic Law), like the play-actor on the stage. Such an identification then would be, as Ramana Maharshi put it: 'like the remnants of a burnt rope'.

You cannot cut off the involvement. It is the understanding – the Source – which cuts off the involvement.

The Source manifests Itself as sentience by extending Itself in conceptual 'space' and 'time'. In this conceptual space-time universe, the Source apparently divides Itself into a subject experiencing an object. In the conceptual manifestation, the Source as sentience brings about discrimination through subject-objet relationships between interdependent opposites as 'acceptable and unacceptable', 'beautiful and ugly', 'good and bad', 'happy and sorrowful'. It is only through non-discrimination, the acceptance of duality as the basis of this conceptual phenomenal universe, that the Source heals itself back to its noumenal wholeness.

THE ULTIMATE UNDERSTANDING pp. 163, 72, 56, 45 & 34

SPIRITUAL PRACTICE

Sadhana can bring about only quantitative changes (such as becoming more loving or less cruel), and it is only the 'pure understanding' of What-Is (all there is, is consciousness in which appears the totality of manifestation and its impersonal functioning) that can bring about the qualitative change (from the relative to the Absolute). This understanding, being of noumenal nature (and not phenomenal or intellectual), brings about the qualitative change through merely witnessing all thoughts, feelings, desires as they arise, without getting involved with them, without identifying with them,.

The more there is the wanting to change this state of affairs, the more running away there is from the What-Is, the more the 'me' is aware of what it feels it lacks. It is only when the mind-heart yields to the existing situation without any fear or hope, and accepts it unconditionally, that the understanding or transformation happens.

CONSCIOUSNESS WRITES p. 9

Every seeker, at one time or another, is plagued by the question as to which spiritual practice he should follow. He does not realize that actually he does not have the free will to choose any particular spiritual practice: he must have the natural tendency towards that particular practice, otherwise the effort would be wasted. Nevertheless, the question remains about which practice is the best. Here Lord Krishna gives the answer.

It may be that a particular aspirant, for various reasons and circumstances, is only able to repeat continuously for a certain length of time a particular ritual or a prayer. Even that, in the circumstances, would be good enough – better than nothing – because, as the Lord has stressed in an earlier verse, no spiritual practice can ever be wasted.

But instead of mere mechanical repetition, if there is a certain concentration of the mind, it would be even better. Better than concentration would be absorption in God throughout the day. 'Absorption in God throughout the day' does not mean to the exclusion of all other activity, which would be most impractical. What is meant is that you should keep Him in your heart always: this means a true conviction that all there is, is God or Totality, which prevails all the time. But above all, says the Lord, the shedding of the sense of doership is ultimately the absolute necessity. So long as there is a sense of personal doership – I am doing the practice of repeating the prayer, I am invoking God or I am doing the meditation – the practice would be of a lower order. Only when there is the deepest conviction that all there is, is consciousness – that only God's will prevails and there can be no personal will or effort – only then will peace prevail.

THE BHAGAVAD GITA p. 94

By continuously repeating a *Japa*, or a Mantra, either as one word or a combination of words, you intend to 'protect' something. What does one want to protect? Something that one 'loves' most. What does one love most? Something which one 'needs' most. And what is it that one needs most? Something without which nothing else has any meaning, any value. Is it not the 'animus', the sense of animating presence, the consciousness, without which you cannot know anything or enjoy anything? This most precious 'need' is consciousness which you want to 'protect' at any cost, and the best way to protect anything is not to be away from it at all. Is it not?

So, the main purpose of repeating a *Japa* continuously is to remain one with consciousness all the time. But you must understand that this 'practice' will enable you to achieve your 'purpose' only for the limited duration while you repeat the *Japa*. A clear apperception of your true nature, on the other hand, is not at all based on the concept of time; apperception is intemporality.

POINTERS FROM NISARGADATTA MAHARAJ p. 174

Before going to sleep at night, spend about ten minutes sitting relaxed both in body and mind, taking your stand that 'you' are not the body-mind construct but the animating consciousness, so that this idea will impregnate your being throughout the period of your sleep.*

Doing Sadhana means assuming the existence of a phantom. Who is to do Sadhana and for what purpose? Is it not enough to see the false as false? *The entity that you think you are is false. You are the reality.*

Once it is understood, or rather, apperceived intuitively, that an entity is purely a conceptual notion, what remains is merely a re-integration – Yoga – in universality. Nothing remains to be done because there is no one to do it and, more important, no one to abstain from doing it either! What remains is pure non-volitional 'being lived' because relatively we are only puppets in a dream-world being manipulated in the original dream. It is for the individual dreamer to awaken from his personal dream. And this apperception is itself the awakening!

POINTERS FROM NISARGADATTA MAHARAJ pp. 104 & 95

My concept is that all 'doing' is not done by any individual doer, but that the doing happens, according to God's Will or according to a conceptual Cosmic Law, which no human being can ever really know because of the simple fact that a created object cannot ever know the basis on which God's Will or The Cosmic Law functions.

Some event gives rise to a thought or desire to do a particular 'sadhana' or spiritual practice. Depending on his natural programming, the seeker decides to do the practice. The apparent free will of the seeker can extend only to the making of this decision. Whether the decision turns into an action, and whether the action results in the anticipated results depends entirely on the Will of God or the

* Ramesh in his talks began to advocate as his Sadhana that at the end of every day, for twenty minutes or so one should analyze two or three main events of the day and honestly see if any 'me' as a 'doership agent' was responsible? Or did everything just happen? This exercise is not in his written works. [Ed.]

destiny of the body-mind organism concerned. If this basis of all action is not accepted, the 'success' of the spiritual practice concerned will almost certainly lead to a certain amount of pride in the supposed practitioner.

My point is that the very thought of wanting to do a particular spiritual practice is not in the control of any individual. Therefore the further progress of that thought into actual doing leading to a particular result certainly cannot be in the control of any individual.

In my own case, I did start the practice of meditation and the practice of repeating a *Japa* (mantra), in the early stages of the seeking. At some point of time, the practice of 'doing' the practice stopped, and the meditation and the *Japa* began to 'happen' – not at any specific times, but at odd times. I have noticed that these days I happen to get up at around 5 a.m., and after the usual morning ablutions, I find myself sitting in my usual rocking chair. The rocking begins but stops automatically, frankly I do not know when! Then the meditation happens – just sitting quietly, watching the breathing getting shallower and shallower – and then suddenly I find that the 'meditation' has stopped after about 50–60 minutes. Then I find myself walking briskly along the length of the apartment – 35–40 steps – until I find, after about 40–45 minutes that breakfast has been served. And thereafter the day just rolls on: the morning satsang (talk) from 10 to 12; lunch; nap, and so on.

When someone asks me whether he should meditate, my usual answer is, 'yes if you like to meditate but I wouldn't force myself to do so.'

LETTER TO ADVAITA IN ULSTER, NEWSLETTER FOR THE ADVAITA FELLOWSHIP, SUMMER 2001

The realization that *sadhana* can bring about only quantitative changes, and that it is only the 'pure understanding' of What-Is (all there is is Consciousness in which appears the totality of manifestation and its *impersonal* functioning) that can bring about the qualitative change. This understanding, being of noumenal nature (and not phenomenal or intellectual) brings about the qualitative change through merely witnessing all thoughts, feelings, desires as they arise, without getting involved in them, without identifying with them. Such witnessing, because of the disassociation with the phenomenal occurrences, brings about those glorious moments of noumenality – the I Am – which become more intense and more frequent as the understanding becomes deeper during the gradual process of 'deliverance'.

CONSCIOUSNESS TO CONSCIOUSNESS p. 17

SPLIT-MIND

It is essential to see clearly the difference between the true understanding in the whole mind and the conceptual understanding in
the split-mind. The whole mind or pure mind is not tainted by the
separation between a 'me' and the 'other' and the thought produced
in the whole mind is, therefore, also pure while the thought produced
in the split-mind is first tainted by the division between the 'me' and
the 'other' and then corrupted by the desire of the 'me' to score in
competition with the 'other'. The whole thing appears to be an
enormous joke when there is the 'Great Awakening', the full realization that life is a living-dream, the entire phenomenal manifestation
of the universe (including all the 'me's' and the 'you's') being merely
an illusory structure reflected in consciousness and cognized by consciousness.

The illusory split of the mind – the content of consciousness –
arises through the attempt of the consciousness to be both itself and
the individual psychosomatic apparatus with which it has identified
itself, a split between its real subjectivity and the pseudo-subjectivity
of the ego, which arises from such identification, a split between what-
we-are and what-we-*think*-we-are.

The illusion ends and the split is healed when there is realization
of this fact, and mind ceases to act from the standpoint of the
conceptual 'me' (in opposition to the 'other') making the constant
effort to control, to choose, to judge.

Such realization comports the understanding that the moon does
not have its cool brilliance because of any special outside treatment,
that the blue mountains are not blue because they have especially
been so painted, that the grass grows by itself and does not need to be
pulled out of the ground, that our physical organs work by themselves
without conscious direction.

We have discovered that the horizontal succession of time, the sequential duration* is a consequence of the single-track verbalization of our split-mind which does not grasp the outer world instantaneously but interprets it perversely by grasping bits and pieces of it and calling them things and events. And this split-mind, with its conscious thought and imperfect perceiving, does not realize its almost total irrelevance concerning the spontaneous working of the psychosomatic organism with its heartbeat, its breath, its complicated nervous system, glands, muscles and sense organs. The comforting thought is that *understanding is all*. The split-mind can heal itself into its original wholeness – and holiness – as soon as it stops grasping because they are not different, the former being only a specialized activity of the latter in order to carry out the working of everyday life. The split-mind must keep its place and restrict its activities to its specialized or technical calling. Only understanding can accomplish this; any effort would only be an effort of the individual illusory entity operating through the split-mind.

All actions and movements and events are extensions in the conceived structure of space and time in order that they may be sensorially perceived and measured in duration, but they all happen in consciousness, exactly as in the dream. The significant point to be understood and remembered is that consciousness, in which everything happens like a dream, is also the dreamer; this is the subjective and dynamic perceiving aspect of the static consciousness, while the objective aspect is the perceived dreamed and discriminated element. In other words, the dream that is the phenomenal manifestation occurs in consciousness, is perceived and cognized in consciousness and is interpreted by consciousness through the duality that is the basis for all phenomenal manifestation. This duality, it

---

* As Immanual Kant and Schopenhauer stressed, space, time and causality are a priori functions of the brain, the organ of cognition, and create the world of representation or illusion. Time does not exist except as a concept, nor space, nor cause and effect relationships. [Ed.]

must be constantly remembered, is merely the mechanism or the instrumentation through which the manifestation occurs (and is of course a concept) with the result that the perceived can be nothing other than the perceiver, the subject (not the pseudo-subject which is also an object) and the object, inseparably united when unconceived and unmanifest, only *appear* as dual and separate when conceived in the phenomenal aspects that totality occurs. All thought and all phenomena are based on the concept of space-time, and since space-time is not some perceptible or cognizable 'thing', it must follow that the perceive-ING and cognize-ING – and indeed all functioning in general – must be noumenal. As the sage Jnaneshwar puts it, subjectivity and functioning are like 'sky and space, or wind and movement, or flame and light'.

The non-action in the no-mind state is not generally apprehended in its true significance; on the contrary, it is misconstrued as idleness in a society where what is approved and expected is a furious competitive spirit in order to achieve a particular goal. But what is forgotten is that all such thinking and acting is in dualism and even the apparent success 'achieved' thereby is so loaded with an inherent depth of guilt that very soon it seems empty and ephemeral, and the split-mind goes ahunting for more and better success, leading to ultimate frustration and a sense of having wasted one's life. This is the basis of the Eastern concepts of *dukkha* and the world being *anitya* (not merely 'impermanent' but more importantly, 'insubstantial' in the sense that worldly success cannot really be grasped). Indeed it is only when the significance of these concepts or doctrines of *dukkha* and *anitya* is firmly apprehended that mind ceases to grasp itself, that mind achieves its pristine purity and becomes what is known as 'unborn' mind or the 'whole' mind, and the action that is in reality 'non-action' *results* (not deliberately but spontaneously).

The identification of the mind – the split-mind with its own image of 'oneself' – results in a kind of paralysis, as it is never certain what it should or should not be doing at any time, because the image, based on the abstract of the past events, tries to imagine itself in the contemplated action. In other words, constant thinking and objectivizing the future in terms of the past, results in perpetual contradiction and conflict and tension. The only answer is to realize that the conscious thinking process, the ego, is a creation of the split-mind. It is only when the mind is let alone to function in its natural way, which is the integrated spontaneous way of the whole mind, that man can witness its working resulting in a special, undefinable effectiveness and power, which the Chinese philosophy of Tao calls 'Te' that can only be loosely defined as natural and spontaneous virtuosity. Such a state of mind, in which its functioning is 'non-active', is called 'no-mind' or 'fasting mind'. It is by no means a state of idiotic vacuity; on the contrary it is precisely the opposite of it when the mind, undisturbed by any intruding thoughts or objectivizing, is at its most alert. This state comes about when the split-mind gives up the impossible task of controlling itself beyond a certain limit and surrenders itself in the sense that it realizes the futility of the perpetual operation of the dualism of thought and action, and lets the whole mind take over.

EXPLORATIONS INTO THE ETERNAL pp. 213, 130, 118 & 31

SPONTANEITY

Non-volitional living does not mean not taking medicines when unwell, nor does it mean deliberately not taking evasive steps to avoid an impending danger. To deliberately not do something or to deliberately give up something is basically an act (a negative act) of volition. It is no different from the positive act of doing something. The whole point of non-volitional living is living without a sense of personal doership. This means merely witnessing whatever happens through all body-mind organisms, including 'your' own, without comparing, without judging. Non-volitional living means neither deliberately sitting in meditation (with a conscious or unconscious motive and objective) nor deliberately avoiding mediation because of an inadequate understanding. Both are acts of volition. When the mind is quiet and falls into meditation, any attempt at resisting it is an act of volition, an act of violence. If meditation happens, welcome it, enjoy it. If meditation does not happen, do not hanker after it. This is the attitude of the sage after apperception has occurred.

A DUET OF ONE p. 162

Understanding is spontaneous and noumenal, even the understanding that the compulsive action is also spontaneous. Then the ego annihilates itself because it is exposed as the illusion that it is. This understanding comports the understanding that actions are not those of the ego but those of the 'suchness' of a particular psychosomatic apparatus based on the genes of that apparatus and the conditioning it has received.

At this stage a doubt may arise: if that is so, it means that anyone could do whatever he felt compelled to do: yes, indeed, but then if the understanding is deep and clear, the same attitude would apply to 'others' as it does to 'me', and there should be no complaints about the damage done to 'me' by such actions of the 'others'. Actually a true understanding would not include any difference between the 'me' and the 'other' because the very content of such understanding would include the realization that both are illusions and that only the events have any significance as a part of the totality of functioning and the individual 'doer' is an irrelevant factor. What this means in effect is that one begins to take life as it comes along in a world which seems to have lost all its previous boundaries and barriers, so that there really is no need to avoid false thoughts or seek the true ones – all thought is spontaneous and without substance, a temporary movement in consciousness that is neither to be accepted nor rejected, but ignored so that it disappears as spontaneously as it appeared.

The essence of all spontaneous action that is the genuine consequence of the pure understanding (in which the 'me' is totally absent as the one to understand) is a natural sincerity. It is not often realized that there cannot be the slightest trace of intention or planning in an action that is spontaneous and natural. What is more, spontaneity and naturalness cannot be 'achieved', either by trying or trying not to try! As the Zenrin poem puts it, 'You cannot have it by taking thought; you cannot seek it by not taking thought.' This may again seem to be an impossible impasse, but it is not really so. Effort (or an effort not to make an effort) is based on desire or volition, which itself is an aspect of the 'me-concept' or the ego. It is the split-mind which sees the apparent impasse as such, while spontaneity is synonymous with the absence of the split-mind. Spontaneity can arise only when the split-mind has been abandoned and trust is put in the working of the whole mind. This does not mean that we must abandon our working mind in everyday life, but that we should not put our whole trust into it, to the exclusion of the whole mind. It is an everyday experience that when our 'conscious' mind cannot provide an answer to a problem, the answer comes to us when we 'sleep on it' through the 'unconscious' mind. There has to be the realization of the limitations of the conscious mind so that we do not force ourselves to be unreasonably careful and only conscious of the illusory 'me'; we keep the liberty to have trust in that final authority which makes the grass grow and our limbs and organs to work 'by themselves'. Otherwise, anxiety and self-consciousness will destroy that minimum sensitivity so necessary for decisions to arise.

What actually happens in life is that man attaches undue importance to past conventions, to conscious thinking, to communication by linear signs and mathematical symbols, and not nearly enough to the intuitive 'feel'; far more to the central spotlight vision and not enough to the peripheral vision; far more to the analytical data and not enough to the 'gut-feeling'. It is absolutely essential to understand that it is not at all a question of one *against* the other but really a matter of one complementing the other. What happens now most of the time is that the conditioning of conventionality is so powerful that it smothers spontaneity; and this unfortunately is clearly to be seen in the education of a child, where the stress on abstract, linear thinking combined with social conventions sometimes reaches such a degree of repression of the child's inherent spontaneity of expression that it could do positive harm to the child. What is necessary is certainly not a surrender to a mad urge of caprice, but a rational recognition of an intelligence that does not base itself on the too orderly working of reason and intellect, an intelligence the actual working of which can be clearly seen in our bodies by the way we are able to move our limbs and take our breaths. As someone has put it, 'men are afraid to forget their own minds, fearing to fall through the void with nothing on to which they can cling'. Man is afraid to rely on the spontaneous functioning with which he is naturally endowed, but which gets blocked when restrained in its natural working by any efforts to understand it in terms of conventional techniques.

While spontaneous activity might seem unusual and a matter of astonishment to the average person, it is the normal procedure for the man of understanding. To others it seems that whatever the *Jnani* does becomes successful and they wrongly ascribe this phenomenon to his 'powers' (*siddhi*). His success is actually due mostly to a sense of confidence that arises through a lack of self-frustrating anxiety. At the same time he is perfectly capable, by the same token, of doing something that comes naturally in the prevailing circumstances with a total disregard to convention or consequence or a sense of decorum.

It is for this reason that he is usually an enigma to most people: his actions are unpredictable precisely because they are natural and spontaneous!

EXPLORATIONS INTO THE ETERNAL p. 214, 216, 30 & 212

SURRENDER

We should abandon conceptual thought and forget our anxiety altogether – on Him we shall rest our cares and fears – and surrender ourselves to Him in the faith that He knows best; our individual view would necessarily be a narrow and limited one which may not in the long run be in our own interests. Much as a parent would love to indulge a child, he would not give a bottle of poison to the child to play with inspite of all the fuss that the child might make. An excellent illustration of the limited view of the split-mind of an individual and the whole mind of the *Jnani* could perhaps be found in the fact that at a certain level of magnification the individual cells of an organism would appear to be engaged in a fierce and ruthless battle for individual survival, but if the organism were to be observed as a whole through a different level of magnification, it would be clearly noticed that what appeared as conflict at the lower level was indeed harmony at the higher level.

In throwing the burden of the cares and fears on to Him, we throw away also the illusory individual – the ego – who had quite unnec-essarily assumed the burden, so that not only the existing worries but the very problem of life simply ceases to exist. When conceptualization ceases, the concept of time – the conditioning of the past and the fears about the future – on which it is based also vanishes and we actually experience the present moment in which the whole world is Brahman, in which we see ourselves as mere units for perceiving the universal functioning and not as distinct and separate organisms with supposed independence of choice and action.

EXPLORATIONS INTO THE ETERNAL p. 162

The only true surrender is when there is no 'one' to ask questions or to expect anything. This means surrendering the *total* responsibility for one's life, for all one's thoughts and actions, to a higher power,

God, or Self. Obviously, such self-surrender presupposes that one can not have any will or desire of one's own – which means in effect the acceptance of the fact that there is no individual entity with ability to act independently of God. This actually amounts to a constant awareness that it is only the Self that prevails and that the supposed individual is truly an irrelevance in the totality of functioning. In other words, there is really no significant difference between Self-enquiry and surrender because in both, the 'me' is finally to be isolated and annihilated.

THE FINAL TRUTH p. 177

Let us understand our true nature and abide therein. Such under-standing would comport the necessity of surrendering our false identification with an illusory entity that is supposedly independent and autonomous. The surrender of this ego will remove all volitional desire that is the hunger. Then, thereafter all action will be spon-taneous action without personal responsibility or guilt. Thus, in this abiding in our true nature will arrive perfect serenity.

Our true nature? The universal consciousness, of course – the sense of Presence which prevails in each and every sentient being without any distinction or discrimination, not as an individual entity but the sense of Presence *as such*. It is this universal consciousness that, in another significant *Abhanga*,* the saint addresses as God and sings, 'Wherever I go, you are my constant companion, leading me by the hand; and taking over all my responsibilities and worries you provide constant support for me.'

EXPLORATIONS INTO THE ETERNAL p. 173

Abhangas are devotional poems or bhajans composed by the great Marathi saints such as Jnanashewara and Tukaram. They are chanted daily in Ramesh's home after his talks.

THOUGHT

Thought – thinking in horizontal time – is the trap, but once it is recognized as such, it can no longer function as a trap.

THE ULTIMATE UNDERSTANDING p. 8

Thoughts into words into actions into further thoughts – that is the vicious circle of the *samsara*. Deep understanding reveals that the functioning of the total universe is based on duality and that each phenomenon is actually 'being lived' according to its inherent nature and subsequent conditioning in order to serve as the respective characters in this living-dream. This understanding translates itself in actual life as 'witnessing' which provides the shield against all experiences in duality. Then, the living becomes spontaneous, natural and non-volitional – noumenal. This is all that the concept of 'enlightenment' truly means.

A DUET OF ONE p. 75

Of course you have to think when you are doing something. Even when you know that life is unreal, dreamlike, as almost every Master has been saying from times immemorial, life has to be lived as if it is real. So when thinking about something you are doing, you are not 'conceptualizing', you are not creating images in your mind and therefore such thinking becomes a part of the 'doing'. When I said that thinking was a pernicious habit, I meant thinking which creates images in the mind. A mind creating images is always a split-mind thinking in dualism, thinking in terms of a subject/object, 'me'/'not-me'. Thinking is a pernicious habit because it creates separation as between 'me' and the 'other', therefore conflict, and therefore unhappiness.

EXPERIENCING THE TEACHING p. 29

It is not that thoughts and desires do not arise. The arising of thought-desire in the mind is as spontaneous and natural as the arising of waves on an expanse of water. It is the nature of the mind to produce thoughts-desires and any efforts to suppress this natural phenomenon will not only be a failure but will intensify the trouble. What does happen after the dawning of the understanding is that *the thoughts-desires are not pursued*; they arise and when they are ignored without being followed up, they disappear. In other words, the understanding results in mere witnessing of the process of the arising and disappearing of the thoughts-desires without any involvement. And then gradually the arising of the desires itself lessens both in its intensity as well as its frequency and to that extent increases the sense of peace and the feeling of contentment.

EXPLORATIONS INTO THE ETERNAL pp. 166–7

Maharaj said: 'There is indeed a great difference between thoughts and thoughts. Thoughts which form day-dreaming or thoughts of regret about the events in the past, or thoughts of fear and worry and antici-pation regarding the future are surely very much different from the thoughts which spring up spontaneously from the depth of one's psyche, what one might call thoughts that do not need any argument and interpretation by the mind. The former are to be ignored and avoided; the latter are incapable of being ignored or avoided, because they are essentially spontaneous and im-mediate and basically non-conceptual.'

Maharaj then continued: 'The very first thought "I am" is surely a thought, but one that does not need any argument or confirmation from the mind. Indeed, as the basis of all further thought, it is the pre-conceptual thought – the very source of the mind. Living according to indirect or mediate thought, in a divided, dualistic mind is what most people do because they have identified themselves with a pseudo-entity that considers itself as the subject of all action. But direct or absolute thought is the process by which the Absolute non-manifest manifests itself. Such thought is spontaneous and instantaneous and therefore, without the element of duration which is an aspect of the split-mind. Whenever there is duration the thought must necessarily be an after-thought, interpreted phenomenally and dualistically.

'No spontaneous, non-dual, intuitive thought can arise unless the storm of conceptual thinking has subsided and the mind rests in a 'fasting' state; and such thought obviously cannot know bondage. Instantaneous, pure thought results in pure action without any tinge of bondage, because no entity is involved.'

Maharaj concluded his reply by saying that most religions were originally based on direct pure thoughts. In course of time they degenerated into concepts. And on these concepts has been erected gradually an enormous amorphous structure, made enchanting enough to attract and mislead millions of people.

POINTERS FROM NISARGADATTA MAHARAJ pp. 112–13

TIME

We abolish opposing positions in space by stating that noumenally there is 'neither here nor there'.

We abolish opposing positions in time by stating that noumenally there is 'neither now nor then'.

We abolish opposing positions of 'me' and 'not me' (or other) by stating that there is 'neither this nor that'.

All the three statements between them abolish opposing positions of the thinker in both space and time. But the thinking entity as such remains intact. In other words, while the entity as subject is removed not only from space-time but even from identification with subject-object, *this very removal affirms its existence – who is removed*? There continues to be a 'who' who has been removed from space, time and subject-object identification. Thus while their relative positions have been abolished, space-time-thinker all continue to exist as underlying concepts; and until those remaining objects are further negated, their subject – the entity – remains intact. To put this differently, the usual negation formula 'neither (exists) nor (does not exist)' is thus inadequate and what is needed is a further negation – the 'negation of neither – nor –'.

What is to be apperceived is the basic and fundamental fact that space-time is a mere concept that enables noumenal manifestation to take place and that as 'I' – which is all that we could all possibly be – we ARE infinity and in temporality. Apperceiving this is experiencing the Teaching. 'We' can only experience what we are as 'I' and the fact that 'we' seem to experience the contrasting elements like pleasure and pain is the ineluctable effect of duality, of which the concept 'we' is an intrinsic part. We can truly experience only what we ARE as 'I' – there is absolutely nothing else to be experienced. And the understanding, the apperceiving, is itself the doing, the experiencing.

EXPERIENCING THE TEACHING p. 124

The truth is very much elementary – basic and simple and rather obvious. It is precisely for this reason that it is overlooked. Anyway, it is, as you said, elementary that the space-time element is merely a conceptual medium in which objects can appear. But it is not realized that this space-time element is obviously not something objective to ourselves as phenomenal objects. Space-time is nothing independent to which we are 'bound' but only a sort of mechanical extension that renders us objectively perceptible to subjective perceiving. It is needless to add that *since we are all objects, the perceiving must necessarily be in the totally different dimension of subjectivity.*

EXPERIENCING THE TEACHING p. 80

The point is that one must, willy-nilly, live in the present moment and if one makes a fetish of improving conditions in the future, one lives neither in the apparent present nor in the illusory future. The fact of the matter is that 'time' is only a concept, the future moves into the past leaving no 'time' for the present. There is only the present moment which is eternity when the relativity of time as a concept of measurement is clearly understood.

It is of the utmost importance to realize that there cannot be any prescriptive method to bring about a cessation of 'thinking' for the simple reason that any such effort would emanate from a 'me' that is itself nothing but a concept, a phenomenal presence which must necessarily be absent so that the noumenal presence may be felt. The very best that any prescriptive method can do is to help the apprehension that it is space-time which is the basis of conceptualization; that, therefore, it is space-time that is the primary hindrance to apperception of our true nature; and that it is only by apprehending the non-objectivity of space-time, and thus eschewing both the positive and negative aspects of conceptuality, that noumenality can enter. In other words, so long as there is a phenomenal 'me' making an effort – or making an effort for not making an effort – the noumenal 'I' cannot enter because the situation is not vacant!

EXPLORATIONS INTO THE ETERNAL pp. 212 & 85

Time and space go together.* Why are you able to cognize things? Because you see them. Would you have been able to see things if they had no form? You see things because they have form, volume, because they are extended into space. Let us go a step further: if things were seen in space for a split-second only, would you be able to perceive them? You perceive things, only because they are extended into space for a certain duration (time), and the forms remain long enough before you to enable you to perceive them.

If there were no concepts of time and space (time and space themselves are obviously not objects), 'things' would not be perceptible and things would not be 'things'. If there were no space-time (no past, present and future), how could there have been any phenomena, any events? Please try to understand that both phenomena and time are merely concepts and have no existence of their own: whatever things are seen, or thought of, are merely images conceived in consciousness, the supposed actuality of which is as 'real' as a dream or a mirage. Now do you understand what I mean when I say that all phenomenality is the child of a barren woman?

This point about space-time is so difficult to grasp that even highly intelligent people are baffled and confounded at its complexity and are unable to comprehend its true significance. At this stage he addressed a question to the visitors generally: 'Have the scientists ever gone deeply into the problem of the nature of space-time?'

The consensus is that no scientists had really made a deep study of this problem, but that some of the topmost among them, including Einstein, had come to the conclusion that the entire universe is 'of the nature of thought', and they held that the nature of space-time is really incomprehensible since it crosses the borders of the mind and all human knowledge acquired so far.

POINTERS FROM NISARGADATTA MAHARAJ p. 73

---

* Many popular science writers wrestle with time – Hawking, Ouspensky, Priestley, etc. But time does not exist 'noumenally', it is an a priori concept in the brain, as is space, and creates the play of life on the screen of consciousness. Time is an empiric convenience on the phenomenal level only. [Ed.]

There can be no 'thing' without 'volume', and no volume would be perceivable in the absence of 'space-time'. Space-time is only a notion. The physicist agrees. Therefore, every 'thing' is a concept, an appearance without substance.

THE ULTIMATE UNDERSTANDING p. 11

TRUTH

Y ou can never know the Truth. Why? Because you are the Truth.

THE ULTIMATE UNDERSTANDING p. 11

And yet the fact of the matter is that Truth cannot be described or explained. Truth is 'What-Is' and the acceptance of it. Every word that is uttered concerning Truth can only be a pointer towards it. The understanding of Truth cannot be achieved. It can only happen. And it can happen only when the mind is empty of all thought, of all conceptualization. When it comes, it will almost certainly come suddenly, without any irritation, when it's least expected. And when it comes, it cannot be accepted unless the mind is empty of the 'me' and the heart is full of Love.

The understanding, which is itself Truth, happens only when there is immediate and direct (and therefore 'true') perception. It happens only in the absence of reason and logic, which are in duality. In such understanding the comprehender (the 'me' as an individual entity) is totally absent and the mind is in total surrender. Understanding, as such, can only spring out of absolute silence, the stillness that prevails when action ceases and conflict ends.

The final hurdle preventing the dawn of truth or apperception or enlightenment or awakening or whatever other word that may be used is *identification as a separate entity.* In other words, the individual may intellectually understand the illusory character of the entire universe and everything therein, *but not that of 'himself'*! And that is the true power of *maya*: thinking, perceiving, living from the viewpoint of the illusory phenomenal center.

The final truth, as Ramana Maharshi and Nisargadatta Maharaj and all the sages before them have clearly stated, is that there is neither creation nor destruction, neither birth nor death, neither destiny nor free will, neither any path nor any achievement.

THE FINAL TRUTH pp. 7 & 8

To a certain extent, the simple truth is made mysterious because of the limitations of the word and the language. Language is like a single beam of light that has to be used to light up an enormous scene, and then the entire scene becomes almost impossible of comprehension if it can be shown only small piece by small piece. It is therefore repeatedly asserted by the masters that Reality can only be apperceived by a sudden illumination like lightning. What the artist visualizes as the finished piece of sculpture, the ordinary man can see only as a piece of stone. It is only by removing the unnecessary portion of the stone, that the sculptor produces the final image.

EXPLORATIONS INTO THE ETERNAL p. 232

There is nothing objective about truth, which essentially is pure subjectivity.

The whole process is like a dog chasing its own tail. In seeking a solution to this riddle one must analyze the problem itself. Who is it that wants the proof of Truth or Reality? Do we clearly understand what we are? All existence is objective. We all 'exist' as objects only, as mere appearances in the consciousness that cognizes us. Is there really any proof that 'we' (who seek proof of Reality) ourselves exist, other than as objects of cognition in someone else's mind?

When we seek the proof of truth, what we are trying to do is equivalent to a shadow seeking proof of the substance! Maharaj, therefore, urges us to see the false as false, and then there will be no more looking for truth. Have you understood what I mean? he asks. Do you not *intuitively* feel what the position is? *That which is sought is the seeker himself!* Can an eye see itself? Please understand, he says: Timeless, spaceless, not cognizable sensorially is what we *are*; temporal, finite and sensorially cognizable, is what we *appear to be* as separate objects. Consider what you were before you acquired the physical form. Did you need any proof about anything then? The question of proof arises only in relative existence, and any proof provided within the parameters of relative existence can only be an untruth!

POINTERS FROM NISARGADATTA MAHARAJ p. 21

ULTIMATE UNDERSTANDING

The ultimate understanding is:

1   That there is only ONE source, pure subjectivity, by whatever name known, Noumenon, Absolute, Consciousness, Primal Energy, or – as the common man would prefer – God.

2   That the phenomenal manifestation is an emanation of, or the reflection of, the ONE Source, consisting of thousands of species of three-dimensional objects, extended in space-time.

3   That, therefore, the human being is one of the species of three-dimensional objects – a sentient object, with the different senses, through which the functioning of the phenomenal manifestation happens – what we know as LIFE.

4   That 'life', as we know it, in the functioning of the manifestation, happens because the primal energy, functioning through the billions of human beings, produces through each one of them, every instant, whatever is supposed to be produced according to a conceptual cosmic law that has prevailed since the beginning of time, the basis of which the human being, a three-dimensional object, could not possibly even imagine, let alone 'know'.

5   That the human being is essentially a uniquely programmed instrument (genes with the unique DNA, plus the environmental conditioning which every human being receives at home, in society, in school, in church or temple) – a programming over which the human instrument could not possibly have had any control.

6   That the very basis of the phenomenal manifestation is the existence of interconnected opposites of every conceivable

variety, beginning with male and female, beautiful and ugly, good and bad and everything else.

7 That the very basis of life, as we know it, is the choosing by the human being between the many interconnected opposites; and being happy if the chosen alternative happens and being unhappy if the other alternative happens. Therefore this comparing and choosing and judging is the basic cause of human suffering.

8 That this comparison and choice cannot be made by the three-dimensional object, and, therefore, the Source had to create an EGO by divine hypnosis, a thought which identifies the ego with a particular body-mind organism and a name, *together with the sense of personal doership.*

9 That, therefore, it is the ego, a mere thought created by divine hypnosis, which is the human being considering himself as an independent entity doing actions and feeling responsible for those actions. All there is in fact is only a three-dimensional object – an animal without any intellect and a human animal with intellect, but, nonetheless, only an object who cannot 'do' any choosing or acting. It is this non-existent EGO – a mere identification with a particular form and name – which considers itself the doer, and, therefore, suffers.

10 That the suffering of the human being is entirely based on this sense of personal doership and personal responsibility, and therefore, the only way the human suffering can be eliminated is by the removal, totally, the annihilation of the hypnosis of personal doership.

11 That the basis of the human suffering is, because of the sense of personal doership, the load of guilt and shame, and pride and arrogance for his own actions and an additional load of hatred and malice towards the 'other' for his action which has harmed him in some way or the other.

12 That the only way to remove this monstrous load on the mind is to be able to accept totally what the Buddha has put so succinctly and so powerfully: 'Events happen, deeds are done, but there is no individual doer thereof.'

13 That the only way this can happen, that the hypnosis of the sense of volition and personal doership is annihilated, is if that is what is supposed to happen according to the cosmic law – or the will of God.

14 That the only thing a human being can 'do' is to investigate thoroughly and honestly who this 'me' is, who thinks he is the doer!

FROM AN ARTICLE IN WATKINS REVIEW
MARCH 2002

UNCONSCIOUS

What are the characteristics of the unconscious thought, and how does it operate? Qualitatively, it does not differ from what is known as whole mind (as opposed to the mind that is split by the duality of subject/object), the potentiality of all thought, because the conscious perception of the present reality by the unconscious thought, although limited to those vibrations which reach the sense organs, is nonetheless a direct manifestation of the whole mind; it is not corrupted by the exercise of any choice or volition by any personal structure. Unconscious thought, or direct thought, is the process of objectivization of what-we-are, which constitutes the apparent universe and maintains it in the apparent seriality of temporality. This direct or unconscious thought, a multitude as differentiated from a multiplicity, evanescent as the *kshana* (split-instant), is a glimpse of eternity. On the other hand, conscious thought or conceptualization is characterized by the personal identification of 'me' with a particular organism as a separate entity together with the dependence on duration for its existence. Conscious thought or conceptualization cannot take place unless the central character of all such thinking is a personal entity and the thinking relates to the outer world only in so far as it concerns the 'me' over a certain period.

Unconscious thought is without duration because it is instantaneous though, of course, it may appear continuous through incredibly rapid renewals; conscious thought on a particular aspect would stop the projector (and the rapid renewals) and remove the stationary 'shot' from the apparent reality of the scene into an imaginary film of its own. Concrete proof of this would be found in one's everyday experience of watching a play being acted on the stage. To the extent that the mental images reproduce faithfully what is happening on the stage, there is no conscious thought as such, but off and on while watching the play, the mind wanders and certain images are fabricated, either having some relevance to what is happening on the stage or even none at all. Such conscious thought is imaginary thought, a fabrication of images which is totally removed from the apparent reality.

EXPLORATIONS INTO THE ETERNAL pp. 128–9

UNDERSTANDING

The great moments of ecstatic harmony arise when there is no conflict, when there is no division between the thinker and the thought, between the observer and the observed, when thought does not bring about a dichotomy between the 'me' and the 'other'. A deep understanding of this fact is all the 'action' that is necessary because then the body relaxes, the mind expands beyond the dualism of the 'me' and the 'other', the heart is free from the fear of failure. Harmony prevails. Then, thought ceases to demand and seek experience and merges in the experience-ING; detached from the rigid and immovable center of the 'me' and its demands and desires, the experiencing is a beautiful free movement without any limiting boundaries. Harmony then prevails because, without preventing thoughts concerning the necessary technical knowledge and daily work, the mind, freed of 'me' and its desires, is free to move in boundless space. Harmony means absence of conflict; it means stillness and silence, peace and tranquility. Such silence is the silent pulse of the universe, the immeasurable vital energy of the universe which exists without any cause, without any reason (a fact which science accepts unconditionally). Such stillness and silence is the absence of the 'me' (and therefore of the dualism), of the illusory ego, and its imagined fears. And such stillness and silence comport the realization that all that exists is the *totality* of the manifested universe and its functioning, that the individual is an intrinsic part of that totality, merely an appearance in consciousness but endowed with the sentience that enables it to perceive and cognize other appearances in consciousness, and that therefore such a mere appearance cannot possibly have any independence or autonomy, nor any volition or choice of decision and action.

EXPLORATIONS INTO THE ETERNAL pp. 77–8

The essence of the ultimate understanding is contained in an extraordinary transformation in the vision of life. In it the usual separation
between 'me' and the 'other' is healed so completely that the organic
unity of the world is not a mere intellectual inference but a deep and
lasting experience. It is not just a belief but a confirmed faith.
However, one must realize that this sense of unity is *not necessarily*
demonstrable in practice. While there may not be a desire to embrace
the beasts and reptiles, there is certainly a firm conviction that our
feelings about the creepy and the slimy creatures are feelings not outside ourselves but 'the hidden aspects of our own bodies and brains'.
What is realized is that the sense of unity is not 'a sort of trance in
which all form and distinction are abolished, as if man and the universe merged into a luminous mist of pale mauve'. There is
understanding that the wide variety and multiplicity seen in the universe are not warring opposites but complementaries like the various
organs and parts of the body. The conditioning of separation, caused
by thought-words, is seen for what it really is. What was an inexplic-
able puzzle to logic and reason becomes a ridiculously obvious matter
of What-Is.

The essence of the ultimate understanding is to see the What-Is as
the manifested expression of the unmanifest reality. It is seeing with
the whole mind of the present moment here and now, without any
effort to make life mean something for the individual in terms of the
future.

THE FINAL TRUTH pp. 224–5

The understanding of the Teaching becomes the experiencing of the
Teaching. The annihilated do-er remains annihilated, and, knowing
the source of our phenomenal appearance in space-time to be what we
noumenally are, we experience the living-dream to its allotted span
in peace. More accurately stated, there is no 'we' to experience the
living-dream. There is only EXPERIENCING of the living-dream.

Maharaj had nothing to teach other than the understanding that there
is no entity to be 'liberated' or 'awakened' or 'enlightened' by any

193

Teaching. It is the beginning because unless there is apperception of this fundamental truth, all Teaching, methods and practice are not only a waste of time but only serve to reinforce the illusion of such an entity. And it is also the end because the apperception of that is itself the only enlightenment there could be.

EXPERIENCING THE TEACHING pp. 133–5

The perfect understanding, then, that is the floodlight vision of the whole universe, shows it as a harmony of intricate patterns, 'a network of jewels, each reflecting all the others'. It is only the spotlight vision that sees each pattern by itself, section by section, and concludes that the universe is a mass of conflict. Indeed, the biological world is certainly a 'mutual eating society' in which one species becomes the food of another, but then it is part of the universal intelligence that that should be so if the whole biological balance is not to be upset by overpopulation and self-strangulation. Actually, it is again the limited spotlight vision which would give this perfectly normal universal phenomenon a sense of horror whereas the broad perspective of the perfect understanding would see things as they really are, that birth and death are really nothing but the integration and disintegration, the appearance and subsequent disappearance, of the phenomenal objects in manifestation.

In other words, true understanding sincerely accepts human failings not only as part of the working of the totality of the universe but as a necessary part like salt is to food. When it is realized that true understanding does not distinguish between proper and improper, right and wrong, but accepts whatever is as the reflection of the noumenal being, it would be clear that any deliberate effort to 'improve' anything would be a self-contradiction. As Maharaj would say, any deliberate effort is like 'beating a drum to seek a fugitive', or as a Taoist sage would say 'putting legs on a snake'. In other words, the basis of the understanding is the acceptance of the wide variety in the multitude of manifestation, the realization of the futility of trying to iron out all differences into a single concept of what is conceived as right or proper, the realization of the foolishness of trying to place the world on a Procrustean bed of linear regulations by stretching a person who is too short for the length of the bed and cutting off a portion of the legs if he is too tall!

When the perfect understanding arrives, it does so along with the realization that there cannot be any separate individual entity to do any deliberate action: it includes the understanding that the individual is merely a phenomenal appearance in consciousness and, as such, cannot have any independent or autonomous existence, and that therefore the ideas of an individual entity having any choice of decision and action is ridiculous. This can lead to only one conclusion that, strictly speaking, all action is spontaneous. This conclusion is demonstrated in life by the fact that very many events do not turn out to be according to preconceived plans. There is also the fact of life (that is quite often totally ignored) that most of the actions that take place in a living organism are entirely without any conscious direction. The difference between the man of understanding and the ordinary man is that the former has trust in the intuitive floodlight vision whereas the latter prefers and chooses to use his limited spotlight vision which, he thinks, he can direct in any direction he wants. The whole point is, however, that in the totality of functioning spontaneous action will take place irrespective of the conceptual volition or intention. Indeed when such acts happen, the individual cannot explain – and he is puzzled – why he apparently did something that was not only not planned but almost wholly against his nature and temperament.

Explorations into the Eternal pp. 218–20

WITNESSING

'Witnessing' has already been referred to a number of times, but this extremely important element of Ramesh's teaching can hardly be overemphasized.

The master key is witnessing without trying to find out any significance to the event concerned, which in effect means dissociation from the event.

In such witnessing – without any analyzing – the ego will be absent.

In witnessing there is full awareness of whatever is occurring in the mind, regardless of whether it is perceiving, feeling or thinking, and such awareness is utterly free of any personal involvement because of the absence of the ego. And when the ego is absent and there is nothing to witness, this state is often referred to as the 'I AM'.

There is a natural movement – smooth and spontaneous – 'upwards' when some event occurs to witness; and 'downwards (deeper)' when no event occurs (to take awareness upwards) for some time, and you sink in the I AM.

Witnessing, because of the dissociation with the phenomenal occurrences, brings about those glorious moments of noumenality – the I AM – which become more intense and frequent as the understanding becomes deeper.

All that now remains is to witness the 'progress' of this process. Who witnesses this progress? Consciousness, of course.

CONSCIOUSNESS WRITES p. 12

YOGA

The point that Ashtavakra makes is that to try to become a *yogi* merely because of being impressed by the looks and deeds of a *yogi* will not succeed. It is only when a *bhogi* (one who enjoys sense-objects) is convinced of the hollowness of it all that he becomes ready to become a *yogi*. Ashtavakra implies first a *bhogi* and then a *yogi*. Until the *bhogi* is ready to be a *yogi* he will be afraid of the knowledge, especially if he has seen a friend violently transformed from one who had a zest and lust for life into someone who is no longer interested in the good things of life. It is only after personal experience yields a deep conviction that the mind is ready to turn inward to its true nature.

The word '*yogi*' used by the sage in these verses needs some explanation because it is likely to be misinterpreted as someone who has *achieved* Self-realization through yogic practices and disciplines. The sage makes it clear repeatedly that by *yogi* he means the one who has transcended the duality of opposites and who has the knowledge with total certainty and conviction, of the illusoriness of both existence and non-existence.

A DUET OF ONE pp. 104 & 147

In *Ramana Hridayam,* Ramana Maharshi says:

The Quest, Who is he to whom belong actions, separateness (from God), ignorance or separateness (from Reality), is itself the Yoga of action, of devotion, of right understanding and of mind control. That is the true state (of the Self) — the untainted and blissful experience of one's own Self — where the seeker, the 'me', being demolished, these eight have no place' (the four defects and the four remedies of Ashtanga Yoga).

The four Yogas are based on the false identification of the seeker with the ego, which results in the attributing to the Self one or the other defect that appears in himself. The Yogi of Action pursues his yoga with the intention of neutralizing the actions of the Self as the doer of actions. The Yogi of Devotion proceeds on the basis that he is someone other than God and needs to become united with Him by devotion. The Yogi of Right Understanding intends to remove from the Self the ignorance which he thinks has enveloped the Self. The Yogi of Mind-Control considers the Self to have been separated from Reality and seeks reunion by the control of the mind.

These are wrong assumptions because the very fundamental truth is that the manifestation of the universe is itself an illusion. The individual self is merely a part of that illusory world. In other words, the Self has always been free and perfect, without the faintest taint of bondage. The seeker of the Self starts with this knowledge and through the quest, *experiences* the true Self. And in the total absence of the 'me', there are neither the four defects nor the four remedies prescribed by the four Yogas.

THE FINAL TRUTH p. 197

EPILOGUE

Once the mystery that is no mystery is fathomed, once the open secret is realized that all that is, is Unicity – whether manifest or unmanifest – one returns to the source and remains where one has always been without the other.

Ultimately there is the sudden realization that all there is, is Consciousness, that all that has happened, and is happening, and will happen is because of God's will and not because of the efforts of the fictitious 'me'. This sudden realization, itself because of God's will as God's Grace, means enlightenment or awakening.

Finally, let us remember Ramana Maharshi's divine words: 'It is as it is. That is all you can say.'

APPENDIX

Autobiographical Notes

The most important event in my life has been meeting a Self-Realized *Jnani* – Nisargadatta Maharaj – in November 1978. It was through reading an article about him in the October issue of *The Mountain Path* (the magazine published by Ramanashramam of Tiruvannamalai, South India) that I came to know of him, and knew instinctively that meeting him would be the most significant event in my life. He lived in one of the by-lanes of Khetwadi in Bombay. When I climbed up the steps into his loft-room in the small apartment, he was sitting at his usual place on a large thick cushion on the floor, a small old man of about 80. When I made my obeisance to him, he turned his penetrating gaze on me, and said quite distinctly in Marathi (the only language he knew well), 'You have finally come, have you? Sit here', and he indicated a place close to him in front. There was no doubt but that in this very first meeting I felt the full impact of his personality and the manner of his greeting – we had never seen each other before in this life. He died three years later and so my actual association with him extended only for a little less than three years, but the impact of it could not have been more intense if the time had extended over thirty years. It would be an understatement to say that my whole attitude to life changed radically in those three years. The most important thing I learnt from him, so far as this life is concerned, is the supreme importance of apparent ordinariness, the unassuming anonymity which is like the natural protective coloring of an animal or a bird. Such ordinariness is not the assumed humility which is in fact actually obsequiousness but rather what is left after the artificiality of the world is realized and therefore shaken off, a virtue that happens to be virtue because it is based on an inner conviction and not something artificial based on the expectation of a future benefit. Such inner conviction comports the acceptance of the ultimate uselessness of competing against others – if you win you become the constant target of all and suddenly, if you lose, you are termed a failure not only by others but, worse, by yourself.

At this stage I must acknowledge the influence which another remarkable person had on my mind over an extended period of time, and that is one Shri Hari Vinayak Gurjar, a teacher in my school. One of his teachings which has remained unforgotten is that if one must compete, one should compete against oneself – the best way of shortening a line is to draw a separate one longer than the existing line! When I found what a wonderful thing it is to be associated with a *Jnani* like Nisargadatta Maharaj, I at once thought of Shri Gurjar who would benefit a great deal by meeting him. Unfortunately, however, Shri Gurjar was then very ill and could not meet Maharaj.

The ordinariness which Maharaj seemed to advocate leaned towards an acceptance of whatever life offered without trying to force anything, which is the basic principle of judo and aikido, which is 'rolling with the blow' or 'swimming with the current', like water following gravity and, if blocked, flowing around the obstacle or finding a new outlet. Such an attitude is healthy because it does not lead to anxiety; because it necessarily involves seeing the universe as a harmonious whole, with the full realization that looking at it in bits and pieces means avoidable conflict; because it underlines the fact that it is an exercise in futility to seek security and happiness (in the sense in which the word is usually understood) in a world where every species is the prey of some other species, where indeed every incoming and outgoing breath involves the creation and destruction of thousands of 'lives' though they may not be perceptible to the naked eye.

After passing my B.A. (Hons.) examination in Bombay, I went to London to join the London School of Economics. There was an entrance examination in which I had to appear for a paper in economics for which there was no specific curriculum. So there was nothing really to cram or mug up except to go cursorily through a book on the subject. When the question paper was distributed, I found that there was a fair amount of choice and I selected general topics where the principles of economics could be applied and not much relevant information as such was required. Also, the answers would be more in the form of an opinion arrived at by applying the principles of economics in a logical, rational manner. At any rate, I happened to write the answers in a relaxed frame of mind, perhaps because I had gathered that the test was more to weed out the sub-marginal applications rather than to test the caliber of each applicant. I had also come to know that for those who, like me, had applied for entrance to the B.Com. (Bachelor of Commerce) course, having previously done a B.A. (Bachelor of Arts) course and therefore not having done any course in accountancy, the usual standard marking was 'partial exemption' from the first year course (prior to the B.Com.) so that one could carry on for the B.Com. course subject to appearing successfully for the accountancy paper at the next examination. Then the results were ready, and I was supposed to see one Professor Plant about my result. When I met the Professor and gave my name, he went through the list and said 'full exemption'. I was taken aback and thought there was some mistake. I explained that in India I had done a B.A. and not a B.Com. He referred to his list again and repeated 'full exemption'. He held out his hand and we shook hands. I came out of his room rather dazed and told my friends that I was given 'full exemption'. They would not believe it, and said there would probably be a correction in due course. But there was no correction, and I am probably the only B.Com. in the world who never appeared for a paper in accountancy! I did, of course, study accountancy later on but not for appearing in any examination relevant to my B.Com. degree. I gathered subsequently that my answer papers for the entrance test were considered so outstanding that the council had recommended full exemption.

What did I learn from this incident? First, that there is such a thing as being in exceptional 'form' which happens at odd times when one cannot do anything incorrect or put a foot wrong, that at such times one finds oneself in complete tune with the universal pulse, the body and the mind work in total relaxation, there is no thought (let alone anxiety) about what might happen; there is only Sheer Joy in the performance itself.

A similar thing happened when once I played a round of golf with the club professional. It was the first day of my vacation and I had left all my worries at the office, and when I stood at the first tee, I had the most fantastic feeling of being at the peak of my physical condition. There was, of course, no question of winning or losing – either losing face or losing money. When we returned to the clubhouse, I had had my best round ever, and the professional did not have to tell me that he had to play quite seriously so as not to lose face by being defeated! Later, on reviewing the game, I found that I had learnt a lot that day. First, that the best results come about (are not 'achieved') if there is concentration on the work itself, that is to say, what is being done, whether it is a ball being hit or a report being prepared or whatever; that concentration does not mean tension; that, on the contrary, concentration means utter relaxation, that relaxation comes about when there are no disturbing thoughts about the results of the effort being made; that, in fact, if there is real concentration and relaxation, the actual effort turns out to be effortless like the winning effort of a champion or an expert in any field; that such effortless effort denotes joy being experienced in the effort itself irrespective of the success which such an effort might or might not result in.

On my return from England after acquiring the B.Com. degree from London University, I had the good fortune to join a leading Indian bank – as a clerk! It happened to be the bank's policy at that particular time not to recruit people, however highly qualified, direct into the officers' cadre, but to promote people from within the clerical grade. I sat at the counter, and did all the work that was expected of a clerk. I was promoted to the officers' grade as soon as there was a vacancy; and, although at times I could not help wondering if my joining as a clerk was not an unwise step, on the whole I became reconciled to the fact that it had certain advantages. In the event of any disagreement or difference of opinion between the clerks and officers on any matter, the argument could not be thrown at me that I could only see one point of view. I could take a dispassionate view. Apart from this inherent advantage, what did I learn from this incident? Most important, I learnt that one must accept in life the bitter with the sweet, that every fact usually has both advantages and disadvantages, that this particular circumstance gave me an opportunity to test myself about the quality of my clerical work; that, in short, one must play to the best of one's ability any role allotted to one on the stage of life. It is not likely that life would be one long continuous road with roses all the way!

FROM THE APPENDIX TO
EXPLORATIONS INTO THE ETERNAL

As I was translating Shri Maharaj's talks into English, I began noticing in my translations the distinct influence of Wei Wu Wei's use of the English language in his books. I have no doubt that traces of this influence would be clearly noticed by the discerning reader in these articles. Apart from the language, it seemed to me a wondrous demonstration of the universality of the subject itself that the writings of a scholar and practitioner of the Tao philosophy like Wei Wu Wei, thousands of miles away, (and hardly a popular writer), would find corroboration in the words of a Self-realized Jnani like Shri Maharaj, whose education as he says himself, takes him just beyond the limit of illiteracy!

Against my better judgement, under pressure from several well-wishers, this paragraph was dropped: the argument was that what I was in effect doing was to place a mere writer on the same level with Maharaj, a Self-realized Jnani.

Perhaps the omission was a mistake – I now think it was – but it did happen, and I suppose it had to happen.

The whole story is that Wei Wu Wei's The Open Secret was given to me as a present by a friend of mine more than a decade before I started going to Maharaj. When I first read it, I couldn't make any sense out of it, except that I had the sense to realize that this book was a real treasure; and I kept it aside so that it might not get thrown out with other books during one of the clean-ups. And for some un-fathomable reason, I suddenly thought of (more accurately, the thought occurred concerning) the book, almost immediately after I started visiting Maharaj. I cannot describe to you the innumerable intellectual frustrations I went through between the two of them – Maharaj and Wei Wu Wei! I felt that the two of them had ganged up to have a private joke of their own, at my expense!! It was indeed a gang-up but, as I realized some time later, it was to bring about an awakening in this body-mind mechanism that was named Ramesh.

When I was first reading Wei Wu Wei (I must have subsequently read the book more than a hundred times – certain phrases and whole lines used to come out of my lips when translating Maharaj's talks), I used to marvel at the command of the English language which a Chinese man should have achieved.

It was some time later that I gathered that W.W.W. was not a Chinese but a wealthy Irish aristocrat (Terrence Gray), highly educated at Oxford university, an authority on wines and race horses.

I got this information through a lady who used to visit Maharaj. She later sent me a photograph of W.W.W. with her. He was a giant of a man. She mentioned Pointers to him, and he expressed a desire to see the book. I would have sent him a copy if I had known his address. I did this as soon as I heard from this mutual friend. I sent a copy to him at his villa in the south of France with a letter expressing my gratitude for the guidance I had received from his book. Unfortunately at that time (W.W.W. was almost 90 years of age) senility was beginning to set in, but his wife read out the book (Pointers) to him and, in his lucid moments, he indicated that he enjoyed the book. Our mutual friend told me that he referred to Pointers as 'Wei Wu Wei without tears'.

Some years ago I was told that Wei Wu Wei is dead. His writings together with Maharaj's teaching helped me enormously. But many people find his writing too abstruse.

Apart from the several reflections that were Ramesh's notes as he was reading Wei Wu Wei's books, the writing for this book happened over a period of a few months. That the writing happened through Ramesh's hand, that Ramesh was not 'some-one' doing the writing, was astonishingly apparent at the time, and is perhaps reflected in the extraordinary nature of this book. During the process of the book being compiled, Ramesh would attentively read various passages with interest, amazement, or even amusement, as if he were encountering these pages for the very first time, altogether new and fresh. It could not be mistaken that there had been some writer 'Ramesh' doing the writing – clearly, the writing had happened.

FROM *THE ULTIMATE UNDERSTANDING* pp. 2–3